Strong Calm Confident You

How to stop the endless cycle of pleasing, perfecting and performing

Kelsey Buckholtz

DEDICATION

This book is dedicated to Mom, Mimi and all the women who paved the way. You have done the hard work of building a future for women where we can be anything we want to be. Now, it's our job to seize it. To Blake, Amelia, my future daughter(s), and the next generation of women, may you be strong, calm and confident; may you live authentically with true happiness in your hearts.

CONTENTS

Acknowledgments   vii

Introduction: The Treadmill   1

Part One: How Did We Get Here?

1   Pleasing, Perfecting and Performing   6

2   Next Stop, Burnout City   13

3   It's Not Them, It's You   17

Part Two: Stop the Endless Cycle

4   Love Your Body   29

5   Care for Your Mind   44

6   Stress Less, Love More   57

7   Self-Care for the Soul   69

Part Three: Embrace Authenticity

8   What Matters Most   81

9   Protecting Your New Life   87

10   Women Supporting Women   99

Conclusion: Pass It On, Sister   103

Where Do We Go from Here?   106

About the Author   107

Notes   109

ACKNOWLEDGMENTS

A special thank you to…

My husband Chris, for your unwavering support in everything I do. You are my rock and I could not have done this without your love and encouragement.

My mom and dad, who instilled in me that I could do anything I set my mind to. You have always been my biggest cheerleaders.

My best friend, Brittany, for your help and encouragement when I was feeling stuck.

My Mimi, for my creative genes and your words of wisdom; and my Uncle Keith, for teaching me what true happiness is and reminding me what matters most.

My coach Lisa Lewis, for giving me the kick I needed to get writing and for guiding me along the way.

My boss Kaitlin, for being supportive of this side hustle and for your guidance around managing my career and life stuff, too.

My Beta Readers, Ashley, Arlene, Brittany, Erica, Gabi, Sandi and Shikha, who bravely volunteered to read the first, messy draft. Thank you for your suggestions to make the book even stronger.

My editors, Whitley Harris and Sarah Sheppard, for your patience, guidance and kindness throughout the process.

My cover-designer Kelsey Martinez for her creative genius and my beautiful cover!

My friends and family who asked about the book, who liked every social media post or reached out to say a blog post resonated. Your words of encouragement kept me going in times of doubt, writer's block, and indecision.

My "SCKuad" – Ashley, Becca, Brittany, Danny, Jared, Jaron, Josh, and Tylee – for your love and support of this dream of mine. You guys are the best crew anyone could ask for.

INTRODUCTION: THE TREADMILL

I had all the things that should have made me happy - a good job, a loving marriage, supportive family and friends. But at the end of the day, I was overwhelmed, anxious and exhausted. I was chasing goal after goal, each time thinking the next milestone would be the one to make me happy. "I'll be happy when I get a promotion, when I have a family, when I make more money," and on and on. But nothing ever felt like enough. *I* never felt like enough. I was overwhelmed with expectations and responsibility, trying to find my place in the world. I was running in all directions of my life, not realizing I was on a treadmill going nowhere.

When I graduated college, like most seniors entering the "real world," my entire life was uprooted and changed in an instant. I decided to pursue graduate school and a fellowship program, as a way into the Fortune 50 company I had interned for. I also moved in with my boyfriend, Chris, in a new state where we didn't know anyone, all within a matter of months.

There were so many new aspects of life tugging me in all directions that I didn't know where to focus. So, I gave 110 percent in everything. While pursuing my master's degree, I was working part-time for my company, working my ass off, taking on every assignment thrown my way and putting in extra hours to prove myself "worthy" of a full-time position. At home, I took ownership of the cooking, cleaning and our social calendar, trying to prove I was "wife material," as if I had to be a 1950s sitcom housewife in order to get a ring on my finger. In grad school, I knew my grades didn't matter nearly as much as they had in undergrad, but I agonized over papers and assignments, still stuck in a perfectionist mindset that straight As were the only way to achieve my goals.

But when everything is a priority, nothing is.

To the external eye, people thought I had it all together, they probably thought my life looked perfect. In reality, I was anxious, depressed and dangling on the edge of burnout. I was a perfectionist, chasing an impossible standard I had built up in my mind of what a woman should be. I was a people-pleaser, trying my best to gain everyone's approval to validate my self-worth.

I thought I needed a better way to manage my stress and that I was doing something wrong. But the only thing that was wrong was the way I treated myself. I learned to numb my feelings with alcohol and food, and as a result I came to hate my body and the extra pounds I had put on since college. I neglected my own needs to please everyone around me, refused to ask for help, and hid behind a mask of perfectionism. I was running on a treadmill, trying to reach an impossible goal, stuck in an endless cycle of pleasing, perfecting and performing.

To break free from the cycle, I had to learn how to love myself again – body, mind, and soul. I started by prioritizing my physical health, learning to take care of and love my body. I focused on my mental health, learning how to deal with my stress and anxiety, and I started practicing self-care to nourish my soul and protect my energy. With this foundation of self-love and confidence in place, I was able to set new priorities and boundaries to live a more authentic and happy life on my terms.

Today, I am strong, calm, and confident. I trust my intuition and I'm finally comfortable in my own skin. I feel like I've taken off the blinders that had me running in place for so long. It's been a journey, and I continue to grow every day, but I am truly happier than I've ever been – and I want that for you, too.

As I did the work on myself, I realized many women are trapped in this cycle of pleasing, perfecting and performing. I started noticing that most women around me were either complaining about all their responsibilities or pretending, like I had, to have it all together.

I see you, and I want you to know it doesn't have to be this way.

What if you could ditch what you think is expected of you – from society, your family, friends, and coworkers – and start living an authentic life on your own terms? What if you could stop trying to be perfect and just be enough? What if you could focus on the things that matter most in your life and let the rest go? What if you could get off the treadmill and jog through life enjoying the scenery? What if you could be confident, trust your intuition and love yourself exactly as you are?

I decided to write this book because I saw the women around me struggling like I had. The chapters that follow detail the experiences and pressures I've felt as a woman and how I learned to love myself again. I'll teach you the strategies and tactics that helped me stop the endless cycle of pleasing, perfecting and performing – so you can start living.

This book isn't a quick fix. It's not a weight loss plan or a "three-steps-to-ultimate-happiness" book. It's not meant to be a quick read or collect dust on your bookshelf; it's meant to be highlighted, dog-eared and referenced. This journey is incredibly personal, and you need to put in the work to change your own life. The tools and exercises throughout the book are ones you can come back to over and over again, and that I hope you'll want to pass on to other women and girls in your life.

We each need to set the standards and the expectations for our own lives and denounce the outdated ones we've become prisoner to. When we do this, together, we can change the story for the next generation of women. When we call bullshit on the "perfect standard" we've been upholding, we help give other women the chance to live authentically too.

It starts with you, and now all you have to do is turn the page. You've got this.

HOW TO USE THIS BOOK

As you embark on this journey in the pages that follow, you will find journal prompts and exercises throughout each chapter to help you apply the concepts from this book to your own life.

To guide you through this process, I've created a free companion workbook. Inside, you'll find the book exercises and prompts, plus bonus content you'll only find in the workbook. You can print it out and write in the space provided or edit the file on your tablet or PC. The book is where the inspiration happens, but the workbook is where the *change* happens.

Whether you complete the prompts as you go or return to them after reading the whole book, it's critical to take pen to paper. Journaling is like having a heart-to-heart conversation with yourself, and if you're serious about changing your life, you need to put in the work.

Download your free companion workbook to get started at workbook.strongcalmkelsey.com/download.

PART ONE: HOW DID WE GET HERE?

1. PLEASING, PERFECTING AND PERFORMING

Women are raised to be perfectionists and people-pleasers. We are taught to be "good girls," while boys are brought up to be tough. We are told to be polite, kind and to always put others first.

In the pursuit of being the "perfect selfless woman," we often fall into the trap of neglecting ourselves. As a result, we learn to see our worth in what we do for others rather than in who we are at our core. We want to be liked, to be needed, to be loved and appreciated. We look at other women who seem to have it all together and put them on a pedestal, not realizing many of them are also struggling behind closed doors

For me, that perfect woman was my mom.

My mom spent most of her life taking care of everyone around her. She is a born caregiver. In addition to being a mom, she chose to care for others in her career as a nurse. She also grew up helping to take care of her brother Keith, who was born with Cerebral Palsy. Eventually she and my dad moved him and my mom's mom (my Mimi) into their home to provide better care. When other family members got sick or her friends went through rough patches, my parents took them in too, offering our guest room without a second thought.

As a kid, I thought Mom was a superhero. She took care of everything and everyone. She was always there for me and willing to talk about anything. Even my friends came to her for advice! In

6

my eyes, she did it all, and I never saw her struggle. She is one of the most loving and caring people I know, and I have always admired that about her.

Now that I'm older, we don't just talk about my problems, we talk about hers, too. I realize now that she too struggles with self-worth. Now I can see that in service of others, she often puts herself on the backburner.

Like many Gen X women, my mom was one of the first women in her family to pursue a full-time career outside of the home. When I was born, she was only 23 years old. "I felt pressure to go back to work quickly, but also guilty for not being at home with you," she told me.

When my mom went back to work, she was on the night shift at the hospital. I had colic as a baby and one night, my dad couldn't get me to stop crying. He didn't know what to do, so he called my mom at work. "I couldn't do anything to help," she said, tears filling her eyes. "It made me feel like such a bad Mom." She was torn between two ideals of wanting to have a successful career but also wanting to do everything her mom had done as a stay-at-home mom.

My Mimi gave her some wise advice, "You are comparing yourself to what you had, but Kelsey will not know any different."

Mimi was right. None of my friends had stay-at-home moms growing up. My mom was at every concert, play and sporting event, and I never felt like she missed out on anything because of her job. Looking back, I now realize that she had to make tough choices, but as her child, I don't recall them in a negative light. I only remember how I felt. I felt loved and supported, and I was (and still am!) proud of my mom for the career she chose.

It makes me sad to think about how much pressure my Mom felt back then. If I could go back in time, I'd tell her not to be so hard on herself. I'd tell her she was doing a great job, and that she didn't have to do it all alone.

According to the Department of Labor, 70% of American mothers are part of the labor force today, and 40% of women are the primary breadwinner in their household (DeWolf, 2017). Despite working women being the new norm, many of us still struggle to balance our work and home life. The concept of the 40-hour work week was designed with the assumption that one partner would work (usually the man) and one partner (usually the woman) would take care of the home and children. Nowadays, most families have two working partners, on top of all the responsibilities that come with owning a home and having a family. Women who work often feel guilty for not being at home, and women who stay home feel judged for not working. The perfect standard we're trying to uphold is outdated.

Mothers are not the only women to face these challenges. When I first moved in with Chris, I felt pressure to be all the things my mom and her mom had been to our family. I was unknowingly playing a game of house, while also attempting to balance graduate school and grow my career in public relations. I thought being superwoman was what was "expected" of me as an adult woman, so I kept it up. I was exhausted, unhappy and wondering: "Is this what life is supposed to be like?"

Women are told we can "do it all," so we try desperately to balance everything ourselves, rather than ask for help. We perpetuate the cycle of pleasing, perfecting, and performing, sending a message to other women that they just need to try harder. We unknowingly uphold these perfectionistic expectations and pass them on like a sacred tradition to the next generation.

Perfectionism: What is it?

Mom and I, like many women, were plagued by perfectionism. Perfectionism is defined as having high expectations and being overly critical of oneself (Frost, Marten, Lahart, & Rosenblate, 1990).

There are three dimensions of perfectionism – or different ways it can manifest – self-oriented, socially-prescribed, and other-oriented perfectionism (Hewitt and Flett 1991).

Traditionally, when we think about perfectionism, we are referring to self-oriented perfectionism, which is when an individual puts immense pressure on themselves to uphold high expectations. This type of perfectionism is driven by a fear of failure. The afflicted associate their worth with achievement but are never truly satisfied with their achievements (Hewitt & Flett, 1991).

Socially-prescribed perfectionists, on the other hand, perceive high expectations and judgment from the people around them. They feel that they must be perfect to obtain approval. (Hewitt and Flett, 1991). Um, hi! I honestly had no idea this was a thing, but it definitely rings true for me. This is where perfectionism intersects with people-pleasing, but I'm getting ahead of myself.

The third dimension of perfectionism is other-oriented. Other-oriented perfectionists demand the highest standards from other people. This type of perfectionism can cause damage to relationships and has been linked to narcissism (Nealis, Sherry, Sherry, Stewart, & Macneil, 2015).

Common signs of perfectionism:

- You are an overachiever, always chasing the next goal.
- You have an all or nothing mindset, anything less than perfect is failure.
- You place value in achievement, rather than the process.
- You fear failure over anything else.
- You beat yourself up for unaccomplished tasks or goals.
- You have trouble asking for help.
- You do not take negative feedback or criticism well.
- You procrastinate tasks or work yourself to exhaustion.
- You hold yourself and/or others around you to extremely high standards.
- You place your self-worth in your productivity.
- You need to be in control of a situation.
- You often don't trust others, so you do it yourself.
- You internalize your stress, not wanting to show weakness.

When it comes to women, self-oriented and socially prescribed are the most common dimensions of perfectionism. Both are caused by a lack of self-love and confidence, whether due to internal pressure or perceived pressure from the world around you. Not surprisingly, both are linked with mental health concerns, including depression, anxiety, eating disorders and suicide (Hewitt and Flett, 1991).

Being a perfectionist can feel like wearing a mask. We're so afraid of failure and judgment that we do anything we can to keep other people from seeing our mistakes, our flaws and our truth. We are chronically "fine," focusing our attention on others for fear of being seen.

Ironically, many of us are wearing these perfectionist masks, while simultaneously wondering how other women have it all under control. We look at social media feeds and see happy families, a successful career and a hot body and think, what am I doing wrong? Comparison is the thief of joy, and social media has made our need to compare so much worse than what our mothers went through. We wonder how the hell other women are doing it all and staying sane, not realizing they, too, are wearing a mask, struggling behind closed doors.

People-Pleasing: What is it?

Perfectionism can also be linked to people-pleasing, particularly for those who suffer from socially-prescribed perfectionism, or the perception of high expectations from those around you.

Many people think of people-pleasers as pushovers, who will do anything and everything that's asked of them. While this can be one sign, there's much more to it than that.

People-pleasers focus their attention on everyone around them, rather than facing the monsters within. We jump through hoops trying to please others and be liked, while neglecting our own needs in the process. We are reliant on compliments to make us feel beautiful, smart and *enough*. We worry about what other people think of us and constantly feel judged. We want everyone to like us, love us, and need us. As a result, people-pleasers often take on undue responsibility for other people's emotions and get frustrated when they can't make everyone happy.

Many people confuse people-pleasing with being generous. The difference, however, is that people-pleasing is motivated by a need for validation, due to low self-worth, while true generosity is fueled by shared happiness, regardless of the outcome (Yiu, 2019).

Doing something nice for others gives you a quick hit of oxytocin, which lowers your blood pressure, increases your happiness and reduces stress (Cedars Sinai Staff, 2019). But if your motivation is to please others, the good feeling will be fleeting and can become addictive. While altruistic acts and helping others can make you feel good, they cannot make up for a lack of self-love. A good deed should feel good internally, no matter what the reaction is externally. If it doesn't, it's time to check your motives and see if people-pleasing may be at play.

Common signs of people-pleasing:

- You have trouble saying no.
- You avoid conflict at all costs.
- You play the peacekeeper between others.
- You will do anything for others.
- You are a social chameleon and get along with everyone.
- You need compliments and approval to validate yourself.
- You apologize too much.
- You describe yourself as generous, selfless, or altruistic.
- You often neglect yourself to care for others.
- You take responsibility for other people's emotions
- You can't make decisions without the opinions of others.
- You are always busy.
- You are exhausted, stressed, and/or overwhelmed.
- You worry about what other people think of you.
- You often feel judged by others.
- You avoid conflict and fear upsetting people.
- You want everyone to like you.

For people-pleasers, if we don't get the validation we need, we worry we did something wrong, or we falsely believe we just need to try harder. On the other hand, if someone acknowledges and approves of our efforts, it gives us fuel to keep pursuing the unrealistic standards we set for ourselves.

People-pleasing, like perfectionism, is rooted in self-doubt and a lack of self-worth. We see our value in what we do for others rather than in who we are. If we don't love ourselves, we become dependent on the approval of others to demonstrate our worth.

Reflect: After learning about people-pleasing and perfectionism, where do you see these behaviors playing out in your own life? What perfect standard are you chasing and whose approval do you crave most? Write your response in your workbook. Download the workbook at workbook.strongcalmkelsey.com/download

2. NEXT STOP, BURNOUT CITY

For women, our need to please, perfect and perform can lead to chronic burnout. If you don't learn to deal with these issues, to stop the treadmill and put your feet on the ground, you will eventually burn out. Burnout is serious and if left untreated can lead to mental health issues like depression.

Early on in my career, I developed a reputation for being able to meet impossible deadlines and produce quality work, which followed me throughout my first few years at the company. I was marked as high potential, earning me even more projects and even more stress. I thought I had to keep up at this pace to succeed as a professional. I was constantly on edge, but I didn't want anyone at work to know it, so I kept pushing through.

My stress and anxiety were through the roof. If work was a treadmill, I was running at a full-speed 10, when I could have gotten the job done at an eight. But the people cheering me on, saying "Great job, Kelsey!" gave me the fuel to keep running at an unsustainable pace, worried that if I slowed down, I would fall.

After a few years of this pattern of pleasing, perfecting and performing, I finally hit my breaking point. I was in a new role at my company and felt like a complete impostor. I was struggling to keep up with the work, and I felt like I didn't belong there. I believed I had to prove my worth day after day.

I held it together at work, but I came home in tears multiple nights a week. Some days I'd burst through the front door, kick off my shoes and take my frustration out on the kitchen cabinets while making dinner. Rather than ask for help I acted like a martyr. When Chris tried to talk to me, I'd snap at him and instantly feel worse. On other days, I cried as soon as I got in the car after work, but when I arrived home, I dried my tears and tried my best to act like nothing was wrong. It's cliché but true, Chris knows me better than I know myself and I could rarely fool him.

I felt like a burden, and my biggest fear was that Chris would hit his breaking point and leave me. I can only imagine what it was like for him during this time in my life – not knowing which version of me would come through the door each evening – angry and anxious or defeated and depressed. But even on my darkest days, he was so patient and kind. I wanted to be a better wife to him, but I was trapped in a vicious cycle of never feeling like enough.

I had become a martyr, attempting to do everything at home on top of a demanding job and grad school. Martyrs believe they are acting selflessly, when in reality their motives are selfish. We give ourselves to others due to a lack of confidence and self-love, but ultimately, we are doing it to validate our own worth. When we don't get the thanks and appreciation we need, we become resentful.

We become so preoccupied with being perfect and gaining approval that we lose sight of our own wants and needs. We become what we think we should be instead of who we authentically are and want to be. And that's exactly what happened in my life. Instead of taking a step back to figure out what I wanted, I was chasing the approval of others. But each time I accomplished a goal, I felt empty. I was exhibiting all the signs of burnout, and I knew something had to change.

Burnout

Burnout is an intense state of exhaustion that comes from extreme, prolonged stress.

According to the National Institute of Health (NIH), the concept of burnout was introduced by Herbert Freudenberger, an American Psychologist. When the term was coined in the 1970s, it was used to describe the consequences of "helping" professions, such as doctors and nurses, who sacrifice themselves for others. Freudenberger found these professions had a high level of burnout, which he characterized by exhaustion, apathy and an inability to cope with the stressors. Today, burnout can affect anyone "from stressed-out career-driven people and celebrities to overworked employees and homemakers" (Informedhealth.org, 2006).

According to the Mayo Clinic (2020), the signs of burnout include:

- Feeling cynical about work or your responsibilities.
- Lack of motivation.
- Irritability and impatience with others.
- Difficulty concentrating on tasks.
- Lack of satisfaction when accomplishing goals.
- Poor sleep quality and/or feeling constantly tired.
- Using food, drugs or alcohol to numb.
- Headaches, stomach issues, and/or other unexplained pain.
- Martyrdom, or giving with resentment.

In order to stop burnout in its tracks, we need to address the root cause. As you've learned, both people-pleasing and perfectionism are caused by a lack of self-love and confidence. Therefore, to change our lives, we need to accept that we aren't perfect, and we can't please everyone around us. We must learn to love ourselves from the inside out. Only then can we build a life on our own terms and pave a new path for the women coming behind us.

Loving yourself is a journey. It takes patience, dedication and continued practice. I'm here to be your guide (your Sherpa if you will!). I'll take you through the steps that helped me change my life and that I hope will change yours too. The chapters of this book follow my own journey, but self-love is not a linear process, and you don't need to follow the exact same pattern I did. You can apply the strategies in any order that works best for your life.

Part one has been all about how we got this way. You've learned about people-pleasing and perfectionism, why these issues are so common for women, and how it can lead to burnout if left untreated. In the next chapter, you'll uncover your fears and how they may be holding you back.

In part two, we'll embark on the self-love journey. You'll learn how to love your body, mind and soul. Think of this self-love work as basic training, where you will learn the skills and techniques you need to face your fears and take back control of your life. Why self-love? Because when you truly love and accept yourself, you don't need approval from others. When you finally get off the treadmill of pleasing, perfecting and performing, you can stop chasing unrealistic standards and pave your own path.

With this self-love foundation in place, in part three we'll work to uncover and embrace your authentic self, which has been ignored for so long. We'll do this by identifying your values and priorities and learning how to build boundaries to protect the life you want.

Here's the thing. You *can* have it all, but you cannot do it all alone. You can be a good partner, a good mom, a good friend, and a good employee. But you cannot be in two places at once. Despite what you may think, you are not superwoman. To have it all, we need to ask for help, we need to learn to say "no" to things that aren't a priority, and we need to stop trying to be all things to all people. We have to stop chasing perfection and other people's approval and commit to being *real*.

Reflect: *Write about a time you felt burnt out. What did it feel like? Were there warning signs that you missed? How do you respond to feelings of stress and burnout?*

3. IT'S NOT THEM, IT'S YOU

To stop burnout in its tracks we need to recognize a core truth – the problem isn't them, it's *you*. You choose what to believe and how to live your life, no one else can do that for you.

For years I thought other people were the problem in my life and the source of my anxiety and chronic burnout. I thought my job put too much pressure on me. I blamed Chris for not doing enough around the house. I felt the weight of "other people's" expectations on me to be perfect.

We tend to blame society, our partners, our boss, and our parents for all the "expectations" we perceive, but for the majority of us, the pressure isn't coming from anyone but ourselves. If you've been paying attention, this is socially-prescribed perfectionism, and it's incredibly common in women. We *perceive* pressure from those around us, which drives us to pursue unrealistically high standards for ourselves.

But the problem isn't other people – it's that we don't love ourselves enough as we are.

As I worked on myself in therapy, I realized Chris never asked me to do all the cooking and cleaning, nor did he actually expect it. He was willing to help if I just asked – living together was new for both of us, so we had to set the standards together. At work and grad school, I was often doing more than was needed or expected. I didn't feel worthy of love or success, so I kept running on the treadmill, trying to prove I was.

To break free from the cycle, I had to face my own fears – or "mind monsters" as I like to call them. These monsters tell us we aren't good enough, we don't do enough, we don't have enough, we don't belong. They tell us what a good wife, mom, and daughter should be. They tell us what a woman should look like. The monsters tell us, if we can just do *this thing*, then we will be happy. But then they tell us we can't do it, and we will never succeed. They tell us it's selfish to focus on ourselves. They tell us we aren't loveable and make us feel alone.

While these mind monsters can be pretty brutal, they can't harm you. I like to think of them as a combination of the characters in Pixar's Monsters Inc. and Inside Out, two of my all-time favorite movies. I picture a tiny Sully arguing with Fear, Anger, and Sadness inside my head, fighting for airtime over my thoughts.

Rather than face these monsters, we've learned to stuff them in closets and under our beds, where we don't have to deal with them. We please, perfect and perform as defense mechanisms to keep them quiet. But this only masks the root cause – a lack of self-love, confidence and self-worth – which is exactly what we're going to tackle in the next part of this book.

I feel it's important to warn you, as you start to put in the work to change your life, these monsters will get louder before they can get better. The monsters feed off of our insecurities and our need for approval from others. So, when we stop seeking that validation and start living on our own terms, the monsters say, "Woah, wait a minute what's going on here?"

When I started writing this book, I hired a coach to help me through the process. In our first session, she warned me about the mind monsters, which she called "gremlins."

"When those gremlins speak up, I want you to remember that they are trying to keep you safe," she said. "But you don't want to live in the safe zone anymore."

Change is scary, but you can't grow in the safe zone. When I started seeing my fears as little monsters who were trying to keep me safe,

I was able to tell them, "Hey thanks for looking out for me, but I'll take it from here."

The first step to taming these monsters is to recognize them and the fears associated with them. Once you acknowledge which monsters you are facing, you can learn how to face them. Now, let's examine some of the most common mind monsters that women confront.

Impostor Syndrome: The Fear of Failure

Impostor syndrome is the monster that whispers, "You don't belong here." It leaves you riddled with self-doubt and anxiety. It says, "You can't do this," driven by a fear of failure or rejection.

Impostor syndrome has often snuck up on me at work when I moved into new roles. As I climbed the ladder at my company, my goal had always been to work in PR. In my third role at the company, I finally accomplished this goal. I was doing PR for a brand I believed in, and I was ecstatic. As I transitioned into the role, impostor syndrome started rearing her ugly head.

The mind monsters made me believe I didn't know what I was doing. I was convinced that eventually someone would realize I didn't belong there, that I wasn't qualified, and I'd be fired. Validation from my boss and my peers was the only thing that kept me going. When someone said I was doing a good job, I thought "Oh, thank god!" I had zero confidence without the approval of others. I felt like I was wearing a mask all day at work, trying to keep up appearances. It was exhausting and depleting, but what I didn't realize was that chasing external approval would never make me feel worthy enough if I didn't believe in myself.

Impostor syndrome often comes out when you are growing or doing something new. It wants to keep you safe and small. If you are pursuing a new goal, this voice is going to come up, but that's how you know you are on the right path. When you recognize impostor syndrome for what it is, you can keep plowing forward. The key to fighting back is to know your value and worth, to be your own cheerleader. I had to learn how to give myself pep talks and not be so reliant on other people's approval – all things we'll work on in the next section.

When the mind monster said, *"You don't belong here,"* I replied, "I was hired over other candidates who had different qualifications. They selected me as the best person for the job. I am growing and learning and that is okay. I am in exactly the right place and I do belong here."

As I worked through the first draft of this book and shared content on my blog and social media, those voices crept up again. *"Who do you think you are?" "No one cares what you have to say." "You aren't qualified to write a book." "You are nobody."*

But I prepared for these voices and I knew how to respond. "I am doing this for me." "I don't need validation or approval from anyone." "This dream has been on my heart since I was a little girl." I can't explain the pull I feel to write this book, but I know I was meant for more, and I was meant to do this. The impostor monster is still there, but my passion and determination are louder.

Guilt and Shame: The Fear of Not Being Enough

Guilt and shame are like a two-headed mind monster. They represent our fear of not being enough – not smart enough, not pretty enough, not good enough.

According to the National Institute for the Application of Behavioral Medicine (NIABM), guilt is the feeling of psychological distress that occurs when you do something against your values. There are two types of guilt – healthy and unhealthy. Healthy guilt is a result of doing something objectively wrong. Unhealthy guilt is a result of doing something below your unrealistically high standards. If you steal something that does not belong to you, you may feel healthy guilt until you give the item back or turn yourself in. However, if you suffer from unhealthy guilt, you may beat yourself up for forgetting someone's name, for example ("Guilt vs. Shame [Infographic] - NICABM").

Shame, on the other hand, is a sense of unworthiness or a belief that oneself is inherently flawed. While guilt can have its place, shame has no benefit to us. It is merely a source of suffering. Shame causes us to fear rejection and makes us want to withdraw from others and avoid anything that perpetuates the feelings of unworthiness ("Guilt vs. Shame [Infographic] - NICABM").

Guilt and shame, like impostor syndrome, are rooted in low self-worth. This two-headed monster causes us to seek validation and approval to counteract our own feelings of unworthiness. For me, shame shows up most often in my personal relationships.

Chris and I grew up in a small town in central Pennsylvania. When we graduated college, I was accepted into graduate school at Rutgers University. We moved to New Jersey to pursue my career goals of working for a pharmaceutical company. Despite following my heart, I felt like a bad daughter and friend for being away from home. I kept in touch with friends and family by sending cards, calling and texting. But somehow, in my mind it never felt like enough. I felt like a bad person for wanting to get out of my hometown, for wanting something different for my life.

When Chris and I drove the three hours back to PA, I struggled to see everyone and do everything in less than 48 hours. I stayed up late to hang out with my mom, a night owl, and woke up early to spend time with my dad, an early bird. I tried to spend as much time at home as possible. As a result, I often missed out on seeing friends. At the end of the weekend, I was exhausted. Still, I felt like a bad daughter and a bad friend. I felt shame every time our car pulled out of my parent's driveway, like maybe I could've done more. I lived with my heart in two places for a long time, torn between the life I wanted and the one I was leaving behind.

As an only child, I took a lot of undue responsibility for my parents' happiness during that transition time of moving away from home. I worried about them constantly. That is, until I finally realized their life went on without me. By opening up in therapy about the shame I felt about leaving my hometown, I learned that I couldn't control anyone else's happiness, not even my parents'. The best thing I could do for my parents was to make myself happy. A parent's job is to raise a good human being to send out into the world. Though this transition out of the nest is one of the hardest things a parent can go through, I realized it's also one of the most rewarding. I knew this was true for my parents. Yes, they were sad every time I pulled out of the driveway, but I also knew (because they tell me!) how proud they are to see me live my own life and succeed.

I realized that even if I sat on my parents' couch all weekend, they also had lives of their own. My mom has errands to run, my dad spends time in the garage, with or without me being there. Their world does not stop because I am home for the weekend, and neither should mine. I realized they love having me home, even if I visit for a short time, because it feels like old times to them. When I visit, I probably spend more time at home than I did as a teenager! Once I realized this, I started spending my weekends in my hometown how I wanted. I made my time with family more intentional by planning meals together, where we could really catch up and connect. But I also went to visit friends and my in-laws. I did whatever made me happy in the moment.

As a result of trying to be all things to all people, women are often plagued by unjustified guilt and shame. We take too much responsibility for other people's emotions or things that happen outside of our control.

A telltale sign of the two-headed guilt and shame monster is over apologizing. If someone bumps into you on the sidewalk, do you apologize to *them*? Do you apologize for speaking up in meetings? "Sorry I'm late." "Sorry to bug you." "Sorry I missed your call." "Sorry I can't make it to your party." It's like saying sorry for taking up space! By overusing the word "sorry," we diminish the value of a real apology.

Instead of saying "sorry," try saying "thank you" instead. "Thank you for waiting." "Thank you for listening." "Thank you for the opportunity to weigh in." "Thank you for your call." "Thank you for the invite."

Guilt and shame fester in the dark, so one way to fight back is by speaking it out loud. When I opened up to my mom about how I was feeling, she knew exactly how I felt, because she's been there too. You can't feel shame when you feel understood. While I still feel guilty sometimes, I remind myself that I'm doing the best I can. I cannot control anyone else's emotions, but I can control my own.

Sensitivity: Fear of Judgment

One particularly sneaky mind monster is sensitivity. Many people think of sensitivity as a trait that causes a person to be overly emotional. But sensitivity is an overreaction to a stimulus.

Have you ever become aware of a ticking clock or a dripping faucet and couldn't get the sound out of your head? Are you bothered by bright lights, loud noises or strong smells? If so, you may be a highly sensitive person (HSP) (Aron & Aron, 1997).

HSPs are very aware of the environment around them. This hyper-awareness can include other people's emotions, which can be particularly troublesome for people-pleasers. Because we are so aware of other people's emotions, we are prone to taking responsibility for them.

As a HSP myself, I can attest. I take everything personally. I think every whisper is someone talking about me. Every giggle is someone making fun of me. HSPs constantly feel judged. If someone seems angry or upset, we assume it was something we did. When a friend doesn't text us back, we think they must be mad at us. If this sounds familiar, you might be an HSP, too.

One strategy that has worked for me is to weigh out the facts. When your sensitivity is triggered and you feel a negative emotion, take a deep breath, take a step back and examine the facts. What information amplifies the negative emotion you are feeling? The things that come to mind first for a sensitive person are typically amplifiers – judgments, and assumptions. Write them down and ask yourself, what information de-amplifies the situation? What information might you have missed? What other explanations could there be for the situation?

For example, if you aren't invited to a friend's party on Saturday night, you might feel hurt.

Information that amplifies this hurt might include:
- A mutual friend was invited.
- You invited her to your last party, and she didn't come.
- She must not like you.

Do you see how quickly that escalates into an assumption or judgment about the feelings of another person?

As a highly sensitive person, I tend to jump to conclusions. But once I recognize this reaction, I can usually think of a few things that de-amplify the feelings and offer alternative reasoning.

Information that de-amplifies the feeling might include:

- You are not very close with this friend.
- You have plans on Friday and would rather take Saturday to recharge.
- It is a small party, so it makes sense you weren't invited.
- The party is far away, and you would rather not make the drive.

After weighing the facts, I can easily see there is more information that de-amplifies the situation, which allows me to desensitize myself from the situation and move on. With practice, you'll eventually be able to use this tool in real-time to prevent or lessen your sensitivity triggers.

Sometimes, you'll realize you don't have enough information to weigh out the situation. When this is the case, it's best to go to the source and ask questions. For example, you could ask your mutual friend when and where the party is and who else is invited before you decide how to react.

Similar to guilt and shame, sensitivity thrives in the dark where it can make up stories. I have found it helpful to be open about my sensitivity with people I trust. In my marriage, when I notice myself making up stories, I will voice them out loud with my husband. For example, I might say, "You seem a little off today. I am starting to worry that you're upset with me. What's going on?" This gives him a chance to correct me, "Oh no, not at all, I just had a crappy day at work," is often his answer. And this also gives him a chance to vent and tell me about his day. Most of the time, other people's emotions have nothing to do with us. So, if you feel safe doing so, it can help to check in with the source.

Sometimes, you will weigh out a situation to realize that the majority of the information amplifies rather than de-amplifies. Still, taking the time to review the facts helps us react appropriately and curb our emotional response. For example, if the information supports being hurt, as in the case of the friend's party, a course of action might be to put more effort into growing the friendship.

Like other monsters, the first step to quieting sensitivity is to recognize it. If you feel yourself getting upset, feeling judged or taking things personally, take a step back and examine the situation. Is what you're feeling based on facts? When you feel judged, it can be helpful to remember that you are your own worst critic, and no one thinks about you as much as you do. It's a harsh truth, but an important one to recognize.

Fighting Back

One thing that all of these monsters have in common is that they thrive in the dark. They hide in corners, in closets and under beds where they can keep us afraid and small. But once we turn on the light, we realize they're not that scary at all.

Ever since I was little, I have always been a scaredy cat. I don't watch horror movies; I'm terrified of spiders and I won't step foot in a haunted house.

My friend Michelle was the same way. In high school, one afternoon, we visited another friend who worked at a haunted house at a local amusement park. She urged us to go on the ride, but we both refused. When her peer pressure failed, this "friend" (if you can even call her that!) took matters into her own hands and pushed me and Michelle into the seat of the moving ride.

After a desperate plea for help, our friend threw us a flashlight. Michelle and I wrapped our arms around each other in fear, and our rickety cart slammed through the front door of the haunted house. *Gulp.*

Michelle kept her eyes closed, but I clutched the flashlight, hands shaking, and pointed it around the room. My fear began to dissolve as I laughed at how stupid some of the "scary" skeletons and ghosts looked in the light. I urged my friend to open her eyes, and soon we were both laughing at how silly it all was.

The key to facing our fears is bringing the monsters into the light, by speaking them out loud and being vulnerable. When we do this, we take away their power.

When I started writing this book, I did it in the dark. I had started a blog as a way to test out content before I published it in the book, and I was working on growing a social media following. But while I had a good following of complete strangers, most of my friends, family and co-workers had no idea about this project. I had worn the mask of perfectionism for so long, I was terrified people would see the real me.

As I told my writing coach about my fears, she said it seemed like telling friends and family about my blog and book was symbolic to me. It was a way for me to dispel the people-pleasing and perfectionistic beliefs that were holding me back.

My coach encouraged me to open up to my loved ones and lead with vulnerability. I'd start conversations with phrases like "I've been afraid to tell you because..." By voicing what you are afraid of, directly to the source, you make it very difficult for that fear to become a reality.

After a few positive conversations, I worked up the courage to post about my book and my blog on my personal Facebook account. Everyone was not only supportive, but genuinely excited for me. This exercise gave me the confidence to fully embrace my dream and start manifesting it.

The mind monsters tell us to be afraid of things we know aren't real. By being 100% authentic and realizing that nothing bad happened, I made that fear go away. It was a much bigger thing in my head than it was to anyone else, so putting it out in the open was a huge weight lifted off my chest.

Mind monsters are really good at making you feel alone. But we all have these thoughts to a certain degree. It's important to recognize these fears and how they impact us so we can learn to fight back. The monsters mean well, but if you don't train them, tame them and learn to silence them, they can take over. If left untreated, these monsters perpetuate our perfectionism and people-pleasing behaviors, which can ultimately lead to burnout.

Reflect: After learning about the various monsters, which ones do you identify with most? Write about them in your journal or workbook. How are they holding you back and how can you start fighting back with vulnerability?

PART TWO: STOP THE ENDLESS CYCLE

4. LOVE YOUR BODY

Now that you understand the causes and effects of pleasing, perfecting and performing, you can learn how to tackle these issues head on. In part-two, we'll learn how to break the cycle by building a foundation of self-love from the inside out – body, mind and soul.

As a young girl, I was always bigger than my friends. My two best friends were both a size 0 and going shopping with them was particularly hard on me. I felt embarrassed as I dug to the bottom of the jean pile, and I longed to share clothes the way the two of them did.

On a weekend trip with one of my friends and her mom, my friend insisted on visiting the hotel gym because of how "fat" she was. I did what friends do, like a scene out of Mean Girls. I objected, "Oh my god! You are perfect – shut up!" I remember looking at her and thinking, "If she thinks *she's* fat, what does she see when she looks at *me*?"

When I was in middle school, my parents went on the Body for Life (BFL) program, a 12-week low-fat, high protein diet and daily workout plan, created by a former bodybuilder, Bill Phillips. Like many young girls, I had started to hate my body, so I decided to join them on their quest to be healthier.

BFL started me on the healthy habit of working out. Every morning I woke up early with my parents to lift weights in our basement gym before school. But what I remember most about this diet is the concept of cheat days. Once a week, we'd indulge in chips, cookies and carbs – all the things BFL deemed "unapproved." As a result, I falsely learned that some foods were good, and some foods were bad.

One day that summer, while my parents were at work, I sat in the pantry on a non-cheat day gorging myself on a bag of chips. I sat on the floor, eating them as fast as I could before the guilt set in. It felt good to "cheat," until it just felt bad, physically and mentally.

The concept of cheat days is self-sabotaging. By telling ourselves we can't or shouldn't have certain foods or that having them means we are "cheating," we only make them more tempting. While BFL helped me learn about the importance of physical exercise and nutrition, it also unknowingly caused me to feel guilt and shame around food, which set me up for a decade of destructive habits.

In high school, I became involved in sports, so I was active and maintained a fairly healthy physique. But still, I felt bigger and less beautiful than my friends. I remember looking in the mirror at my hips and just wishing they could be smaller. I wanted to be skinny like my friends. And this was all before we had social media to compare ourselves to others 24/7.

In college, my issues with my body image continued. A roommate and I attempted to balance our unhealthy late-night habits by going to the gym. I treated exercise like punishment for everything I'd eaten over the prior few days,

To help motivate ourselves to get out of bed and to the gym, we each recorded a nasty message on each other's phones to be our ringtone. It was something along the lines of, "Get out of bed, fat ass! Your thighs are crying from rubbing together!" At the time, we thought this was hilarious, but now I realize it was super messed up! If I recorded a gym reminder for someone today it'd be like, "Hey girl, you look fabulous today. You should go move your body because it feels good and it's good for you. You've got this!"

Thanks to yo-yo dieting and alcohol, I put on about 20 pounds by college graduation. The freshman 15 seemed to have crept up on me slowly. I had no confidence in my body, and I was at an all-time low. I tried to go to the gym, but driven by disgust rather than self-love, I often skipped my workouts and then figured I might as well over-indulge on "bad" foods. I was eating to numb my feelings and working out as a form of punishment. But the problem wasn't what I was eating, it was my attitude. I had to learn to love and respect my body to stop these unhealthy patterns.

Respect Your Body

Does my story sound familiar? Have you been trying to motivate yourself to get healthier by hating yourself? Did you catch yourself naked in the mirror this morning and say something you would never utter out loud to another human being? Do you pinch your skin, examine your cellulite and chastise your reflection for "letting yourself go?" Do you weigh yourself every day, sometimes multiple times a day, only to criticize the number you see? Cut it out, girl! It is *not* okay to talk to yourself and to treat your body like this. Without a foundation of self-love, no diet or amount of exercise is going to make you feel more confident.

There is no "perfect body." The standards of beauty created by the fashion industry change over time. When I was growing up in the late 1990s and early 2000s, skinny was in. Today, on the contrary, many of us want a big booty and a small waist. There is no perfect shape or size and believing there is can be extremely detrimental to our mental health. That's why it's so important to learn to love your body as it is. We are all born in different shapes and sizes and that is part of what makes being a human and a woman so beautiful.

Try This: *Before you go any further, I want you to write a love note to your body. I know this sounds a little cheesy, but I promise you, it's important. In the note, include three things that you are grateful for about your body and three things you love about your body. Make a promise to treat your body with love and respect.*

Dear Body,

I am grateful for all you have done and continue to do for me. Thank you for growing me from a little girl into a woman. I love many things about you, body. Most of all I love your strong arms, your beautiful blue eyes with just a speck of brown, and your powerful booty that carries us through the day. Thank you for keeping me healthy and strong. From now on, I promise to treat you with the love and respect you deserve.

Love,
Kelsey

How difficult did you find this task? If it took you more than five minutes, you've got some work to do in this department. And I get it! I've been there. I've done a lot of work to get to this point of self-love, and you can too. Keep this letter handy as you go through this self-love process, and I promise you it will get easier. Hang it in your closet, on your computer or the bathroom mirror. Put it somewhere you can read it every day until you start to believe it.

Our bodies have done and can do incredible things. They carry us through life and protect us from harm. Mamas, you have literally grown another human being inside you! Don't look at those stretch marks as defects; they are battle scars, and you are a warrior. So, let's show our bodies the respect and grace they deserve.

Rather than beating ourselves up for how we look or how we think we should look, let's learn to be grateful for our bodies and all they have done for us. Starting today, I want you to stop treating yourself like garbage.

In this chapter, you'll learn how to love your body and treat it with respect. I'll teach you how to move your body in a way that doesn't feel like punishment. Then we'll explore how to fuel your body with high-quality energy. Finally, you will learn about the body-mind connection and how to change your mindset around food and exercise

Move Your Body

The first step in learning to love yourself is finding a way to move your body and practice physical activity that you don't dread. The key is to find a type of exercise that you actually want to do.

Exercise should make you feel good! If you love to dance, Zumba may be the perfect option for you. If you are motivated by competition, a sports league might be the way to go. Have you always wanted to run a marathon? Training for a race can be a great motivator. Or perhaps you need the accountability of a personal trainer, which requires an appointment and ensures you're practicing the right form and intensity. Or maybe you're like me and you will love the flexibility of working out at home, through on-demand and digital exercise classes.

Throughout college and post-grad, I continued to slog away on cardio machines at the gym, even though I hated it. Because I wasn't enjoying it, I wasn't motivated and didn't see results. It wasn't until I found Tone It Up workouts for free on YouTube that my healthy habits started to stick. I was instantly drawn to the founders, Karena and Katrina, two best friends teaching fitness right from their own home. I fell in love with K&K's workouts because they are quick and effective. Their high intensity interval training (HIIT) workouts are 20 to 30 minutes, helping me maximize my time. HIIT workouts changed the way I think about fitness and from that moment on, I said goodbye to the treadmill.

There are so many different types of workouts, and I truly believe there is something for everyone. Do some trial and error and find what works for you. Don't force yourself to go to hot yoga just because your friend Amelia loves it, but also don't give up after the first try.

As you consider the best exercise option for you, also think about your personal preferences and your lifestyle. If you're a busy mama or you're just short on time, at-home workouts may be the way to go. If you can't get yourself motivated or if the social aspect is important to you, you might prefer hiring a trainer or attending a regularly scheduled class to give you some extra accountability. As you try different workouts, take note of what you enjoy and what works best with your personality and schedule.

Here are a few options to consider:

- Sign up for a personal training consultation at your local gym. The first session is often free!
- Ask a friend to join you in a free trial class at a local studio/gym - try yoga, kickboxing, barre or Zumba.
- You may prefer lifting heavy weights over cardio! If your friend Blake is into CrossFit, ask if you can be her guest at

an upcoming workout of the day.
- Short on time? Try these at home workouts:
  - Dance workouts by The Fitness Marshall on YouTube.
  - The Tone It Up App, which offers a free trial before you commit to a subscription.
  - Lauren Gleisberg, who has free workouts on her Instagram and plans you can purchase.
  - Have a friend who does Beachbody? Ask if you can try a few of their workouts.

Find something that makes you feel good and stick with it. If you need to spend money to do so, invest in yourself! Why are we hesitant to spend money on things that will benefit us, but we don't bat an eyelash at our Starbucks addiction or the Amazon packages that magically appear on our doorstep every day? Find room in your budget to invest in yourself and your health will pay for itself in dividends.

Now, if you're like many women, you've already started to tell yourself that you don't have time to work out. I know, I know... you have seven kids, plus your partner is like a big child to take care of, you have a full-time job and a side hustle, and you volunteer for three different organizations and your kids' school. You just have too much responsibility! But remember, these responsibilities and expectations are often exaggerated in our own minds. Instead of "I don't have time" try telling yourself "It's not a priority," and see how that feels. Ask for help and take some time back.

I bet if you take a look at how you're really spending your time you can find at least one available hour that you can dedicate to physical activity. If you really can't find the time, I'm going to say something that won't shock you. Wake up earlier! Go to bed at a reasonable hour and get your ass out of bed in the morning. Listen, I'm going to level with you – it will suck for a few weeks until your body adjusts, but you *will* adjust. You must find this time in your schedule for yourself if you want to change your life.

When I started Tone It Up, I was strictly an evening workout person. I was the type of person who needed coffee and food to function in the morning, and I believed there was no way I could work out in the morning. But K&K talked about the benefits of starting your day with a workout (Nunez, 2019) – increased energy, improved mood, fewer distractions and better choices throughout the day – so I decided to give it a try.

As my responsibilities at work and grad school increased, it was harder and harder for me to get a workout in at night. So, I learned how to be a morning person. I set my alarm for 30 minutes earlier, and then an hour and then two hours earlier until I was regularly getting up at 5:30 a.m. I began to love my mornings. Every morning, I wake up and have a cup of coffee, meditate and work out. Working out in the morning sets me up for a much healthier, more productive day because I have already done something good for myself before starting my workday.

Stop telling yourself you don't have time; stop telling yourself you aren't a morning person, or you just can't do it. You can do hard things. Start small and work your way up to your goal. If you want to change your life, you have to make changes – it's that simple.

While prioritizing yourself is simple, it may not always be easy. You may need to have a conversation with your partner or kids to carve out this time for yourself. Tell them why it's important to you and how you plan to accomplish your goal. Making your health a priority is a great example to set for those you love, so have an open and real conversation about it with your family.

Once you allocate the time and find a workout or two that motivates you, aim for three to five days of workouts per week for 30 to 60 minutes each. The time you need depends on the intensity of your workout and the program you're following, but the goal is just to get moving. Even 15 minutes is better than nothing at all.

If working out is completely new to you, start small. One of the biggest mistakes I see people make when they are trying to start a workout routine is going balls to the wall in week one. They get sore, exhausted and defeated. They crash and give up altogether. If you're just starting out, try working out three days per week, giving yourself a day to recover in between. You may want to use those days to stretch or take a walk with your dog. If you do feel sore, know that soreness is a sign that your body is changing! Don't use it as an excuse to stop. Foam rolling, yoga and stretching can help. Make sure you build in time to recover and don't go too hard too fast. Work yourself up to 5 days of 30 minutes of activity per week.

Try This: *Plan to try three to five new workouts this week. Journal in your workbook about your experience and rate, on a scale of one to five, how fun it was, how challenging it was and how motivated you think you would be to do it again.*

Fuel Your Body

Once you've incorporated physical activity into your schedule, the next step is to fuel your body with nutritious foods.

This is not a diet book, and I'm not a nutritionist, so I cannot and should not tell you exactly what to eat. But I can, however, tell you what I've learned from years of dieting, food shame and other unhealthy habits. I'll share what has worked for me – and what hasn't – in the hopes it will help you.

By the time I graduated college, I had tried several different diets to no avail. I continued to struggle with my weight and body image, leading me to overeat and pursue unhealthy choices far too often. My turning point came when a friend posted a picture on Facebook from a birthday party. I barely recognized myself – I was overweight, unhealthy and behind my smile I realized I was unhappy. That picture motivated me to start taking better care of my body.

I had no idea where to start when it came to nutrition, so I pursued yet another diet program: Weight Watchers (now referred to as WW). WW helped me learn how different foods impact our bodies and what nutrients we need to function. Through a mysterious calculation of protein, carbs, fat and fiber, WW assigns a point value to every food. Users are given a specific number of points per day, based on their weight loss goals, body composition and gender. All fruits and vegetables were given 0 points to encourage users to fuel their body with clean, nutritious foods. In recent years, WW updated their calculation to be based on protein, food energy/calories, sugar and saturated fat. Now, the program has over 200 foods that are listed as 0 points.

Similarly to Body for Life, WW offers a method for incorporating less nutritious foods into your diet. In addition to your daily allotment of points, users are given "extra points" to use throughout the week or save up for one day. This concept started to teach me the concept of balance. WW doesn't classify foods as "good" or "approved" versus "bad." Every food has a point value and can be accommodated. That said, you learn pretty quickly that if you eat three pieces of pizza for lunch, you will have a hard time staying within your points for the day without going hungry. WW also taught me that certain foods were lower in points and would keep me feeling full longer, allowing me to conserve points for dessert in the evening. Thanks to their recipes, I also learned how to make nutritious meals and how to make healthier versions of my favorite foods like mac and cheese and desserts.

While WW was a good start on my nutrition journey, the problem was that I could only learn so much. You can read a nutrition label and enter the info into an app to get the point value, but you don't really understand why one food has more points than another.

The WW formula is sacred because it drives their subscription model, so it was tough to maintain my results when I stopped paying for the program. I didn't know how to create a balanced diet without tracking points.

So, I set out to learn more about the science of nutrition on my own.

Macro tracking became the missing piece of the puzzle that helped me understand more about food and nutrition. It also helped me break down some of the limiting beliefs I had built up from years of poor body image and diet culture.

Macros is short for macronutrients, or the nutrients that your body needs and uses the most – protein, carbohydrates and fat. Tracking or counting macros involves calculating your body's individual macronutrient needs and tracking your daily intake of those nutrients in an app or food journal.

You can find tons of information online on how to incorporate this method into your life. Lauren Gleisberg's Macro Book gives a quick and easy overview of how to calculate your macros and how to use tracking to enjoy foods like Doritos and pizza while still maintaining a healthy lifestyle.

It is important to note that this method may not be the right tool for those with a history of eating disorders or if you think the tracking will become obsessive for you. While it may not be for everyone, macro tracking helped me learn how to eat in a more balanced way without self-sabotaging after one "treat." Using the MyFitnessPal app to track my macros, I'm able to incorporate more of the foods I love into my daily meals. If I want dessert, I track it and move on.
I do not track every day, but I use macro counting as a tool when I need to reset or refocus on my nutrition goals. Macro tracking has helped me look at food in an unbiased way, and it can be a useful tool to educate you on what you're putting into your body. With this tracking system, I was able to adopt new, healthier beliefs about food that have helped to stop the shame spiral of self-sabotage.

Self-Sabotage: The limiting beliefs that are holding you back

While I've learned a lot about nutrition from various diets, I've always had trouble managing my sweet tooth. Eating processed, sugary foods increases your dopamine levels. Dopamine is a hormone that's associated with pleasure. The more processed or sugary foods you eat, the more dopamine that's released in your brain and the more you want to eat to experience the pleasure. (Kadey, 2018). That's why processed, less nutritious foods can be highly addictive.

Some studies suggest that if you're suffering from a mental health condition, such as depression, you may be lacking dopamine (Grace, 2016), which may explain why we seek it out through other sources, such as food, alcohol or drugs.

For my husband's birthday this year, I made his favorite dessert: Boston Creme Cake. This isn't something I make regularly, so it was a special treat! I sang "happy birthday" to him and served us both a piece of cake. I ate it so fast I barely enjoyed it, and then I immediately felt shame and disappointment. These feelings made me want to eat another piece.

"You barely enjoyed that; what's wrong with you!?" one of my mind monsters said.
"Maybe if I just have one more piece, I'll enjoy it more," the

Dopamine Devil on my shoulder replied.

"No, you won't; you don't need that."

"I DO need it. I only have it once a year, so I might as well enjoy it. I'll be better tomorrow."

"No, cake is BAD!"

"I have no willpower. I love sugar... I hate sugar."

As I returned to the kitchen to put the cake away, the Dopamine Devil convinced me to have one more bite directly out of the pan, and then another and then another until I felt sick. The next day, I avoided the cake all day until the evening, when I gave in and the pattern repeated itself.

The problem wasn't sugar, it was my mindset. Cake is something I thought I shouldn't have, so I ate it quickly and mindlessly leaving me unsatisfied and wanting more. Every time this happens, it's as if I think if no one can see me and if I eat it really quickly then it doesn't count. I have been trained through diet culture to believe that sugar is "bad" and that I can't control myself. I knew I had to fix this all-or-nothing mindset if I wanted to stop this shame cycle around food.

There are no "bad" foods

In order to stop yo-yo dieting and self-sabotaging, you need to realize and wholeheartedly believe that there are no bad foods. I want to give a shout out to my girl Alex from Fitlicity, which offers Habit-Based Health programs. Working in her small group program was a huge step in my nutrition journey, because she doesn't believe in a one-size-fits-all approach. Instead, she works with each individual to find out what works best for them. She didn't tell me what I could and couldn't eat, but she helped me see how different foods impacted me physically and mentally. I learned SO much from her program about food and the macro- and micro-nutrients that foods provide our bodies. I learned that all foods are nutrients; they aren't good or bad. After spending years restricting certain foods, it was really important, but difficult, for me to make that mindset shift.

I can honestly say that I now genuinely enjoy eating nutritious foods like vegetables. These foods fuel my body and I feel more energetic when I eat clean, whole, real foods. But, here's the thing. I also *love* desserts. I've tried sugar detoxes and all kinds of programs to reduce my sugar cravings because I believed sugar was bad. When I started counting macros, I finally understood that no food is inherently "bad." Now I understand that I can have cake any time I want it, in moderation, within my macros, so there's no need to overindulge in one sitting. No matter what food I enter into MyFitnessPal, the app distills it down into protein, carbs, fat and other nutrients. Unlike WW, I now fully understand how a food impacts my macros for the day; there's no guesswork.

There is no wagon or track to fall off of

In the health and wellness space, and on Instagram specifically, girls talk about "falling off the wagon" or needing to "get back on track" with either their workouts, nutrition or both. This phrase is a pet peeve of mine. I used to be the same way, but I realized this way of thinking is destructive and not productive. This is an all-or-nothing mindset that tells us there is only one path to being healthy, and that's not the case. The "track" you're trying so desperately to stay on is actually a hamster wheel, which is why you're spinning in circles. Get off the wheel and pave your own path! With macro tracking, I'm able to focus on making balanced choices rather than trying to have a "perfect" day of eating.

Eat what makes you feel good

We have been trained through diet culture to feel guilty about our food choices. Guilt leads to shame, which spirals into self-sabotage. Guilt says, "I shouldn't have eaten that." Shame says, "I have no self-control. I'm a sugar addict. I will never change."

Shame tells us that we are inherently bad, which means we can't change, and that's simply not true. When we do something we need to apologize for, guilt is a necessary emotion, but this shouldn't be the case with food. When you remove the word "bad" from your food vocabulary, you remove the guilt.

Focus on how your body feels when you eat certain foods. Eat the foods you want and ask yourself, "Does this make me feel good, or does it leave me feeling bloated, gassy, crampy or uncomfortable?" Either way, no guilt is needed; simply acknowledge, analyze and adapt. If you *do* overeat or eat something that makes you feel crappy, make note of it. Analyze it and change your behavior to make the next best choice you can. Don't wait for tomorrow or Monday to start over. Make a choice that makes you feel proud at your next meal.

Food is meant to be enjoyed

By treating sugar like forbidden fruit, when I did decide to have dessert, I couldn't stop myself. I often overindulged on things that weren't even enjoyable or satisfying to me. I'd eat cake even if it was three-days old, leftover and dry in the kitchen at work.

Learning to eat slowly and mindfully without guilt and shame taught me to enjoy my food and to figure out what actually satisfied me. Certain previously "unapproved" foods were ones I enjoyed, and some were not. Pasta, for example, makes me feel too full, bloated and yucky. Plus, pasta is just not that tasty to me. Warm chocolate chip cookies on the other hand? Hell yes!

My biggest fear was that if I could have dessert any time I wanted I would go hog wild. But that never happened. After a day or two of eating processed, sugary foods my body naturally started to crave vegetables and clean, whole foods because it was lacking in certain nutrients.

The key to maintaining a more balanced lifestyle is to listen to your body, including your cravings. Trust yourself!

You don't need to "cheat" on your diet

As a strict rule follower and perfectionist, I could follow a plan, but I didn't know how to account for anything "off-plan." The Body for Life diet I attempted in middle school, taught me the concept of the "cheat day," and I've had to work hard throughout my adult life to undo this unhealthy mindset. Words matter and they impact how we feel and how we act. You're not cheating, you're just eating

I like to call less nutritious foods "treats" because it has a positive connotation, rather than the word "cheat" which has a negative connotation. A treat is a food I love but know I should enjoy in moderation (like pizza or ice cream), because it provides fewer nutrients to the body and likely won't leave me feeling fully satisfied.

You may have heard the saying "food is fuel," and while we need food to function, it also has other benefits. Food brings people together in celebration and tradition, and it can provide other emotional benefits if you allow yourself to enjoy it. You don't have to abstain from foods you love in order to be healthy.

Macro tracking has finally given me the freedom to eat what I want whenever I want. One choice doesn't have to "ruin" my day. I no longer beat myself up for having a treat, because I can see actual data that one ice cream cone only makes up a small percentage of my macros for the day.

Even after attending a party or having a day that I once considered to be "overindulgent," I often retrospectively put my food into MyFitnessPal and realize that I'm not that far off of my macros for the day. You don't have to abandon all of your healthy habits for the day because of one food choice. Counting macros allows me to give myself more grace. Every choice is your choice, and it's the overall average of your choices that counts.

Similar to exercising, you want to start small with nutrition and focus on adding healthy behaviors rather than restricting or taking away certain foods. Remember not to fall into the all-or-nothing trap. If you try to give up sugar and carbs and only eat clean foods all at once, you're setting yourself up for a pantry binge session.

Pick one item from the list below and work on incorporating it into your week. Then, add one more. Slow and steady.
- Incorporate one fruit or vegetable into every meal.
- Use Pinterest to search for healthier recipes
- Drink half your weight in ounces every day. If you weigh 150 pounds, you should drink 75 ounces of water every day.
- Add more healthy, whole foods into your diet; think unprocessed foods that come from the ground or a tree.
- Give macro tracking a try! Check out LG's Macro Book or research macro tracking on your own.

Whether you decide to try macro tracking or not, I highly recommend keeping a food log in the early stages to make you more aware of the quality and quantity of food you're eating.

You can keep a log on paper or in an app like MyFitnessPal, which is free, but has a premium option as well. I tried to keep a paper log for years but found it difficult because I didn't always have my notebook on me. MyFitnessPal works well for me because I always have my phone.

If you've had history of an eating disorder or you think you may become obsessive, tread carefully. The point is not to obsess over every calorie, but to understand where you're currently at with your diet and what may need to change. However, you also need to be gentle with yourself and show yourself some grace.

With your food log, note how different foods make you feel. You may realize that some food groups don't sit well with you, or you may find that foods you previously thought were "bad" actually give you energy. Despite what diet culture has taught us, no one food group is inherently "bad"; they just may not work for you.

✧◆✧

When it comes to health and fitness, women have been brainwashed by diet culture leading to unhealthy patterns of body shaming, disordered eating and self-sabotage. That's why loving and accepting our bodies must be a priority if we want to change our lives.

Move your body every day and fuel it with nutritious foods because you love your body, not because you hate it. In my own life, learning to love my body and treat it with respect opened up the door to self-love. It's not easy, but it is so worth it.

Reflect: In your workbook, reflect on your why for wanting to get healthier. It's okay if one of these goals is physical but think about the broader picture too. Perhaps you want to be more confident or prevent a disease that plagues your family history. Do you want to model a healthy lifestyle for your children or partner? Whatever motivates you to meet this goal, explore it here. Which of the limiting beliefs around food are impacting you from reaching your goals? How can you consciously work to reframe them?

5. CARE FOR YOUR MIND

Learning to love my body was a good start, but I soon realized I needed to take care of my mental health if I truly wanted to change my life.

I lived with an undiagnosed anxiety disorder for most of my life. It wasn't until my mid-twenties that I realized not everyone worried as much as I did, and I didn't have to suffer and struggle so much.

Anxiety can be both a cause and effect of people-pleasing and perfectionism. It is ultimately a fear of the unknown, and we all experience it at certain points in our lives. Anxiety is characterized by intense worry, nervousness and dread (Mayo Clinic Staff, 2018). It is a biological response to a threat, causing a fight, flight or freeze response (Nunez, 2020). Your heart races, you start to sweat, and your mind becomes singularly focused on the threat in front of you. This response dates back to prehistoric times. When a caveman encountered danger, like a wild animal, the body snapped into survival mode, deciding to run or stay and fight.

Today, we rarely experience danger in the form of man-eating animals, but rather in the uncertainty of everyday life. We may experience anxiety when someone cuts us off in traffic, nearly causing an accident, or when we do something that scares us, like riding a roller coaster or giving a speech.

Often, we experience anxiety around changes or transitions in our lives, or "threats" to life as we currently know it. You might experience worry when starting a new job, sending your first-born off to college, or moving to a new state. These sources of anxiety are situational, and everyone experiences them from time to time. Because we all experience symptoms of anxiety, it's helpful to learn how to recognize and manage it during these stressful times in our lives.

For some people though, the anxiety never goes away. Generalized anxiety disorder is biological rather than situational. Your fight-or-flight response is essentially overactive and perceives threats everywhere. If there isn't a legitimate threat, your brain creates one; it finds something to worry about. Have you ever been so happy that you stopped and worried about the bad thing that must be coming your way? This is one of the signs of generalized anxiety disorder. For me, anything uncertain is a huge struggle.

My Story

According to my parents, I was a very fearful and anxious child. Everything new was a struggle for me and likely more so than the average kid. I cried so hard going to preschool for the first time I had to be picked up and taken home. When I took swimming lessons, I was terrified of the deep end and refused to go in, which caused me to fall behind on my lessons. I went through a period where I was afraid of boys and men. At gymnastics, I bawled because I didn't want to be lifted onto the equipment by a boy. As a child, I had nightmares so terrible that I woke up screaming and wouldn't let anyone touch me.

This difficulty with sleep continued into middle school, when I would lie awake worrying for hours. I worried constantly about doing the right thing, being a good kid and wanting everyone to like me. I also started having intense stomach pains. We went to multiple doctors, had tests and scans conducted, and no one found anything wrong with me. I didn't realize the source of my pain was anxiety all along.

My mom, God bless her, dealt with many confessions during this time in my life, as I tried to cure the anxiety. If she was ever uncomfortable, she never let it show. She always knew what to say to make me feel better. She told me I could tell her anything, and I did! Sometimes I wrote her notes to bring up subjects I didn't know how to talk about, or we had heart-to-hearts in the car. A lot of my worries during this time were the beginnings of people-pleasing and perfectionism.

As an only child, I always wanted to make my parents proud. I wanted to be a good girl, a nice girl, the perfect daughter. I've read a lot about anxiety and people-pleasing and these traits can often surface from childhood trauma or a lack of love and attention at home, but that wasn't the case for me at all. I'm really lucky. I have amazing parents who have always loved and supported me. It wasn't that I didn't get enough attention or praise; it was the opposite. I feared I wasn't as good as they thought I was. I tried to prove to myself that I was worthy of their love and praise by maintaining my grades and being a good kid. I put all of this pressure on myself and it started to become too much.

Around that time, I had learned about suicide from current events and TV shows and had become terrified of the idea of it. I had a friend who I knew was cutting herself, and I was afraid she would seriously hurt herself, or worse. I told my mom, who of course told my friend's mom. She wasn't happy with me, but I knew I had done the right thing.

After that, I became preoccupied with the idea of suicide. I became afraid of sharp knives, scared that I would impulsively and intentionally hurt myself. I didn't want to die, and though I never did anything to hurt myself, I couldn't stop thinking about it. Eventually, these thoughts got so scary, I told my mom.

Though I'm sure she too was terrified by my confession, Mom assured me that it was normal to have these thoughts from time to time. But she suggested that I might want to talk to someone other than her about how I was feeling.

She took me to a therapist who asked a lot of questions and then talked to me about the intrusive thoughts I was having. Intrusive thoughts, I learned, are unwanted images or thoughts that appear out of nowhere. They often involve harming ourselves or others or doing something you would never do in real life. The therapist helped me understand that thinking something doesn't mean it will happen. We are not our thoughts and we don't need to be afraid of them. We can acknowledge the thoughts and let them go. The therapist also taught me strategies to help me fall asleep at night when my thoughts were racing, strategies I still use today (more on these in chapter seven).

I only saw her once or twice, but my first foray into therapy was a defining moment for me in terms of my mental health. Despite how much it helped, I never told anyone about it. Even at a young age, I was embarrassed that I had to see a therapist. I didn't want people to think I was crazy.

Just as I started to get a handle on my anxiety, I started high school. The pressures and worries worsened. I heard stories of freshmen being hazed by upperclassmen, and I was terrified. Once I settled in, I worried about my grades and getting into college. I worried about drugs and drinking. I worried about upsetting my friends. I worried about, well, everything.

On the day of my junior prom, my friend Alison was killed in a car accident. This was one scenario I'd never even imagined in my worst nightmares. I remember the day in bits and pieces like a nightmare, not sure what's real and what I've imagined, blocking out the most painful parts.

At my high school, everyone went to a local garden to take pictures before prom. While there, someone told me they had heard Alison was in a car accident and didn't make it. This was before everyone had a smart phone and social media, so it was just hearsay. I was shocked but convinced myself it was just a bad rumor. My mom encouraged me to go to prom and said she'd try to find out what had happened. Later she told me, she drove by Alison's house that afternoon and her parents were outside talking with the police. As they made eye contact with her, they waved her on, silently begging her not to stop the car. She knew the horrible rumor was anything but – Alison was gone.

My mom showed up at the prom to break the tragic news to me in person. When I saw her, I knew; she didn't have to say anything. I collapsed into her arms, and begged her to take me home, but she refused. "There is nothing you can do right now, and Alison would want you to enjoy prom," she said. But how could I dance and laugh and sing as if something terrible hadn't happened? I spent much of that evening in the bathroom with a few close friends as we held each other. It was not the prom any of us had imagined. It was like a bad horror movie.

After Alison died, I developed anxiety about driving. I was terrified of driving in any bad conditions, but especially snow. Earlier that same year, I had a close call myself when my little Ford Escort slid on black ice, nearly hitting a tractor-trailer. I wondered why my life was spared and Alison's wasn't. If someone forgot to text me when they got home, I'd panic until I got ahold of them. After Alison, I pictured losing every single person in my life, as if somehow, I could prevent it or at least prepare myself by worrying about it.

In a way, all of my anxiety about my grades paid off, or so I thought. I was accepted into my dream school – Penn State University, main campus. But once I was there, I experienced social anxiety for the first time.

I decided to live with a friend during my freshman year. We both had boyfriends going into college, so it seemed like a good idea. But when she dumped her boyfriend a few months in and started dating a freshman on the floor above us, I realized a harsh truth - I hadn't made any real college friends. I joined the college newspaper, the Public Relations Student Society of America and got involved in the Penn State Dance Marathon (THON), a year-long fundraising effort culminating in a 46 hour no sitting, no sleeping dance marathon. But despite joining these clubs, making friends just didn't come as easy as it had in high school.

I found it really difficult to get close to anyone at Penn State because it was such a big school. I didn't know how to make friends and I felt awkward asking people if they wanted to hang out. I remember wanting to be friends with two girls at the school newspaper and feeling so awkward asking for their numbers. It was like trying to date them!

Soon enough, I learned to numb these feelings with alcohol, as I realized that a few shots made me feel a whole lot better, at least for a while. When one drink took the edge off, I had another. Alcohol made me feel more spontaneous, fun and less nervous. Taking shots and playing drinking games became my norm. But I didn't have an off switch.

After a night of binge drinking, without fail, I woke up with a stomachache, a headache and regret. My anxiety forced me to replay everything I did and said in my mind – at least what I could remember. "Oh my god, did I actually say that last night?" "They must think I'm a loser." "Ugh, why did I drink so much." "I can't remember getting home... oh God, I hope I didn't humiliate myself." This cycle continued almost every weekend throughout my four years of undergrad. Drinking alcohol masked my anxiety in the short term but subsequently made it worse.

When I graduated, my anxiety doubled. Outside of the bubble of a college campus, I no longer knew what was expected of me. In school, there were rules and clear expectations – get good grades in order to be accepted into college. In the real world, there were no rules or grades to guide me.

The Impostor Syndrome Mind Monster was particularly loud at my first job. "You'll never get this done." "You have no clue what you're doing." "You're going to get fired." If you had asked my coworkers or my boss, they would have told you I was doing great. But I put pressure on myself to do everything perfectly and not to let anyone see me sweat.

As I climbed the ranks at my company, the deadlines were always tight, with multiple last-minute requests and too many people to try to please. While I always got everything done, the stress was messing with my physical and mental health. My anxiety started manifesting as anger, and on my worst days, depression. I felt shame for taking it out on Chris, and my biggest fear was that one day he'd hit his breaking point and leave me, and this caused even more anxiety. I knew something needed to change. I hadn't been to therapy since I was a kid, but I felt I needed to talk to someone who could help me learn to manage my stress.

I started by visiting a counselor through my company's Employee Assistance Program (EAP), which offered a series of free therapy sessions at the office. I talked to the EAP counselor about my work challenges, but ironically, I was so stressed I had trouble making time for my appointments, even though they were in the building I worked in. I constantly had to cancel or reschedule at the last minute because I was too busy at work. Reg flag!

On top of that, I felt shame for needing this support, which only perpetuated my thoughts that I didn't truly belong in my job. I didn't want anyone at work to see me going into the EAP office, so I snuck out to my appointment like a secret agent on a mission. Remember, shame festers in the dark where it can make you feel alone and worthless.

It was hard for me to open up to the counselor and dig deep into what was causing these issues for me in the middle of the workday. I was afraid I might cry in her office and have to go to my next meeting with a puffy face and red eyes.

After my series of free EAP sessions, the counselor suggested I find a mental health professional outside of the work environment to get more comprehensive support. I used a tool on my health insurance website to find therapists in-network near me. I looked at their websites and chose one that felt good to me. I filled out a request for an appointment online and someone called me to do an intake evaluation to match me with the right therapist.

What Brings You in Today?

If you are going through something right now, I encourage you to book a therapy appointment. Be honest with yourself about where you are. You likely picked up this book for a reason and I truly hope it helps you, but a mental health professional can offer you something I can't: individualized support.

In your first therapy session, you will likely be asked, "What brings you in today?" or in other words, "What is the reason you decided to come to therapy?" Before your session, jot down what you want to discuss ahead of time. I like to keep a running note in my phone..

Think of the first session as a first date. The mental health professional wants to get to know you and you're getting to know them, too If you don't feel a connection, don't be afraid to meet with someone else. Therapy works best when you feel comfortable and understood, so make sure you find the right fit. Talking to a therapist is like talking to a friend if you've found the right one. Only, this friend can listen objectively and recognize patterns in your behavior.

Outside of the work environment, I was able to dig deeper into my personal triggers and issues. My therapist helped me recognize patterns and identify the limiting beliefs that were holding me back. Together, we discovered that people-pleasing and perfectionism were the source of the majority of my anxiety. I was constantly afraid of upsetting people around me. I wanted everyone to like me – no, love me. I wanted to be the best friend, co-worker, daughter, wife, etc., and I put way too much pressure on myself to do it all.

I'll never forget when my therapist said, "It's not your job to make everyone else happy."

She was right; other people's emotions are not our responsibility. *You* are your responsibility. The only thing we can control is our own reactions. Rather than wanting everyone at work to like me, I learned to seek their respect instead. In other words, I began to focus less on doing what I thought they expected of me and started focusing on being authentic and trusting my gut, which helped me gain respect.

This can be a hard concept to grasp after a lifetime of trying to please others. This next exercise can help put it into perspective.

Try This: *Write down three people you respect and admire. Then list all the qualities you value in these individuals. What is it about them that you admire and want to emulate?*

If you struggle with people-pleasing, I'm willing to bet one quality you admire in others is authenticity. Because we tend to morph ourselves in an attempt to seek approval, we look up to those who show up as unapologetically themselves and we respect them for it. So, that's the idea here. You want to show up authentically at work (and everywhere, frankly). Not everyone will agree with you all the time, and that's okay! Rather than being liked for someone you're not, your goal should be to be respected for who you are.

Fighting Stigma by Sharing

For a long time, I never told anyone I was going to therapy, not even my parents or my husband. I didn't want anyone to think something was wrong with me. It felt like a weakness, an imperfection. The stigma around mental health prevented me from talking about it.

My dad was one of the first people I talked to about my mental health because he opened up to me first. As I was telling him about a particularly stressful day at work and how much I was struggling, he took a deep breath and said, "Honey, take it from me. Learn how to deal with your stress now. You can get control of this a lot sooner than I did in life."

He was seeing a therapist, unbeknownst to me, and admitted he'd wished he'd gone sooner in life. He saw his younger self in me and didn't want me to suffer as much as he had.

I told him about the counselor I had been seeing at work, and that I had made my first appointment with a therapist. Opening up about my mental health journey was a real turning point for me, and it deepened my relationship with my dad. Now, my dad and I can connect on a new level. We have a lot of the same tendencies and can compare notes and strategies that help. It's also nice to talk to someone who totally understands how I feel when I'm anxious.

Thanks to my dad, I slowly started talking about my anxiety with other people I trusted. Each time I opened up, I felt relief. Once people knew, I no longer had to pretend, and I could finally take off the mask of perfectionism. The more I talked about my mental health, the more I felt like myself.

Several months into a new job, I went on a work trip with a coworker, who I didn't know well at the time. She mentioned casually that she had a history of anxiety, which inspired me to share my own story with her. Soon, we were comparing notes and she was giving me advice on how to manage anxiety, addressing one of my biggest fears of becoming a mom and how I'd manage my anxiety in that situation. After opening up, we became really close. When I was feeling anxious at work, I could go to her and she'd know exactly how I felt.

I began to talk about my mental health on my social media accounts. Each time I opened up about my experience, people reached out to say, "me too!" When we talk about mental health, we give others permission to do the same, like a chain reaction of vulnerability. Friends, family members and even people I didn't know started reaching out to me to tell me how much my writing resonated and inspired them. These conversations have been the greatest gift along this journey and one of my biggest inspirations to write this book.

There is still so much stigma around mental health, but it is much more common than most people think. One in five Americans suffer from mental illness, which means your family members, your friends and your neighbors are struggling too. I've never regretted opening up to someone about my mental health, and I encourage you to share your story too.

Therapy is nothing to be ashamed of. It doesn't make you weak – it makes you strong. It's weak to suffer in silence, but it takes courage and strength to open up and to seek help. Whether you have a mental illness or not, I can't recommend therapy enough. We've all got our own shit to deal with, so don't be ashamed of prioritizing your mental health. I think everyone can benefit from talking to an objective third party – someone who won't take sides and can remain completely neutral. Therapy helped me level up my life by uncovering the habits, beliefs and behaviors that were holding me back and teaching me strategies to combat my anxiety.

The process of finding the right therapist, and one that you can afford, isn't always easy, but I promise you it's worth it. Many companies now offer an Employee Assistance Program (EAP) which can get you started and also help you with the process of finding help outside of work if and/or when the time comes. You can also visit your health insurance website to find a mental health professional in-network. You can also try an online service like BetterHelp or TalkSpace which can offer affordable options and a super easy way to test out therapy before committing. Think of it as an experiment; try at least three sessions with three different therapists before you decide whether or not to continue.

When Therapy Isn't Enough

Therapy helped me gain control of my anxiety, and I was feeling on top of the world again – until I was promoted at work.

It was a position I *really* wanted; one I'd been working towards for a long time. But it was also a challenging role for me; one intended to help me grow and develop new skills to propel my career at the company.

I was excited and motivated, but I believed I had to prove myself. I felt unworthy and was convinced that one day someone would realize I didn't know what I was doing, and I would be fired. It was a case of impostor syndrome, worse than I'd ever felt before. I felt like I was pretending all day long and when I came home at the end of the day, I felt exhausted and defeated.

I continued to go to therapy, but it was no longer enough. My therapist asked me multiple times if I regretted taking the job, and I always said "no." The problem wasn't the job, it was me. I loved the job and I wanted to succeed, but I felt like I wasn't good enough.

One day, I came home from work so overwhelmed that I got into bed and refused to get out. I felt so defeated. My husband was used to my tears, but this was out of character for me. He sat with me and tried to coax me up, but I was inconsolable. I knew he was worried about me and I hated myself for "burdening" him with my problems, but I couldn't stop crying. Thankfully, he refused to leave me alone. Eventually, he was able to calm me down enough to get out of bed and into a nice warm bath. He truly is a saint.

When I recounted the story to my mom, she suggested talking to my therapist about how I was feeling and looking into medication to get me through this period. She, like Chris, knew this wasn't normal behavior for me.

I went to see my therapist and told her the story in detail. Before I could ask about medication, she said she wanted to refer me to a psychiatrist at the practice who would be able to prescribe me something to get me over the hump of this new job. Silent tears fell from my face as I nodded in agreement. I wasn't sure what to expect, but I knew I didn't want to feel this way anymore.

When I went to see the psychiatrist, I told her about my history with anxiety and what had been going on with my new job. She asked me about my symptoms and took notes. She smirked, knowingly, as if my case of anxiety was "so textbook." And though I felt a little judged, I also felt extremely validated. Her smile told me that I wasn't alone and how I was feeling wasn't as strange as it felt. Her lack of concern told me everything was going to be okay. She put her pen down and looked at me and said, "It sounds like you have Generalized Anxiety Disorder and that you probably have for a long time now."

That was the first time someone told me I had an anxiety disorder. Strangely, it was a huge relief. Tears flooded down my face, like a dam opening up for the first time, I felt instant relief. She told me we were going to try a medication to help take the edge off of my anxiety. I was nervous, but desperate to feel better, so I agreed.

It took a few different medications to find one that worked for me, but eventually, I found one that helped. Once I found the right medication, I felt like a cloud was lifted from my line of sight. While I still had some anxiety and stress (we all do!), I felt like my threshold was raised and that I could see problems and solutions more clearly. I remember going back to the doctor for a follow-up and telling her, "I think I'm getting used to my job and getting more comfortable. I know what I'm doing now and I'm feeling so much better!" She gave me the same smirk she had in our first session and said, "I also think the medication may be working." After that, things got a lot better for me.

I share this story because I want you to know it's okay to need medication for your mental health. If you went to the doctor and she said you have diabetes and you need to take insulin, would you question it? Most likely not. So, if a doctor or psychiatrist recommends you try a medication for your mental illness, I encourage you to be open to it and give it a try. Medication really made a difference for me and completely changed my relationship with anxiety. If something feels off, don't be afraid to speak up. Tell your therapist or primary care doctor about any sudden changes in your moods or behavior.

I cannot stress enough how important mental health is and how transformational treatment – therapy and medication – has been in my life. Today, I am in a much better place. You don't have to suffer in silence. Taking care of your mental health is a critical piece of the journey to self-love. The sooner you ask for help, the sooner you can take back control of your life.

Reflect: *In what area(s) of your life are you feeling stuck and could use support? What steps could you take to improve your mental health? Is there someone you could open up to about your current challenges? Is therapy something you are willing to try? If you are already seeing a therapist, could you ask about medication? What is holding you back from taking these steps?*

6. STRESS LESS, LOVE MORE

Through therapy, self-help books and trial and error, I have learned several strategies and tools to help me manage my stress and anxiety. In this chapter, I'll take you through these strategies and how to use them.

Reframing Negative Thoughts

As you start to add healthy behaviors into your life and do the work to love yourself better, you will start to notice that your negative thoughts or mind monsters may get louder before they get better. But remember, you are not your thoughts! Sometimes these negative thoughts can keep you from being productive and doing what you need to do, which is why it's helpful to learn how to reframe them. Just because you have a thought doesn't mean it's true and it doesn't mean you have to listen to it.

Start by noticing what the monsters are saying throughout the day. When you start to feel triggered, sad, angry or anxious, take a minute to recognize what thoughts are going through your head. You may be surprised to realize how toxic your own thoughts are and how much they may be impacting you.

Byron Katie, a well-known author and speaker, created a method of self-inquiry called "The Work." The Work consists of four questions that anyone can ask themselves to reframe a negative or stressful thought. When you notice a negative thought, ask yourself the following questions:

1. "Is it true?"
2. "Can you absolutely know that it's true?"
3. "How do you react, what happens when you believe it?"
4. "Who would you be without the thought?"

After answering these questions, find what Katie calls "the turnarounds." Ask yourself, "Could the opposite of this thought be true?" (Katie, 2002).

I love this exercise because it gives you an opportunity to recognize the mind monsters that may be clogging your thoughts with negativity. Katie's method allows us to take a step back from negative thoughts and examine them. Considering if the opposite could be true helps us get out of all or nothing thinking patterns that can perpetuate our anxiety.

Here's what "The Work" looks like in practice:

Thought: *"I don't have the authority to write a book."*

Is it true? *"Yes."*

Do you know for sure that it's true? *"No."*

How do you react, what happens when you believe that thought? *"I feel inadequate and unmotivated to continue writing."*

Who would you be without the thought? *"Without this thought I would be more productive, creative and confident in my writing, making the whole process much easier."*

Find a turnaround. *"I don't need authority to write a book because my experience is unique, yet relatable to many."*

Another method I use for positive reframing is to talk to myself with more compassion. What would you say to a friend who voiced this thought out loud? If you are making an assumption about someone or something, what other possibilities could there be for what is happening in the moment?

Thought: *"She seems off today. She must be mad at me."*
Reframe: *"She's probably just having a bad day."*

Thought: *"This is too hard. I don't know what I'm doing."*
Reframe: *"Yes, this is difficult, but you can figure it out."*

Thought: *"Today is going to be a terrible day."*
Reframe: *"Today can be a good day if you choose to make it so."*

It's important to note that there is a difference between reframing toxic thoughts and avoiding difficult emotions. As humans, it's natural for us to feel angry, anxious or depressed from time to time. If you're experiencing a loss or going through something tough, you can't just reframe it away. When you do "the work" and the thought is absolutely true, you should allow yourself to experience these emotions and practice self-care when you're feeling down, which we'll talk more about in chapter seven.

However, if the thoughts aren't true, reframing can help get you out of toxic patterns. Mind monsters are liars. They doubt your worth, they call you names, and they cut down your confidence.

As you start to notice patterns in your negative thoughts, you can also turn your reframing statements into affirmations by making them short "I" statements that apply to many different situations. You can use affirmations proactively to drown out the toxic thoughts by saying them out loud.

Here are some of my favorite affirmations:

- "I am worthy and capable."
- "I am enough."
- "I am in control of my actions."
- "Yes, I can."
- "This is tough, but so am I."
- "I can do hard things."
- "I am perfectly imperfect."
- "I am beautiful."
- "I am a good person."
- "I am loved."
- "This too shall pass."
- "Inhale confidence, exhale doubt."
- "I am doing the best I can."
- "I love and respect my body."

- "I am strong, I am calm, I am confident."
- "I've got this!"

As you get more comfortable noticing and reframing your thoughts, you'll be able to do it in real-time. One day, you'll find yourself in a meeting and a negative thought will pop up, maybe something like, "Don't say that, you'll sound stupid! Who do you think you are?" You'll know your training is working when another voice says, "Wait a minute, that's not true!" and you speak up anyway. The more you practice reframing your thoughts, the easier it will become and the more confident you will feel.

Try This: *Work on noticing and reframing your own negative thoughts.*

1. *Keep a log of all the negative thoughts that pop into your head for 24 hours. These can be thoughts about yourself, others or reactions to situations. What do you say to yourself when you look in the mirror? When you try something new? Write down anything negative the mind monsters say for the entire day.*

2. *As you notice these thoughts, reframe them into positive statements. Examine each thought and ask yourself whether or not it's true, use "the work" and write down a response to each question.*

3. *Create three positive affirmations based on the patterns you noticed. I like to keep a list in my iPhone notes section. When recurring negative thoughts come up, I read through my affirmations and say them out loud if I can!*

Meditation

A meditation practice can help make reframing negative thoughts easier as you learn to train your mind to be more mindful. Meditation is like strength training for your brain. It is a practice of mind-body connection, mindfulness, and awareness. Meditation, at its core, is about separating yourself from your thoughts and feelings. Meditation can give practitioners a better sense of calmness, relaxation and overall psychological balance (NCCIH, 2016).

If you're rolling your eyes and thinking about skipping over this section, I encourage you to keep an open mind. Meditation is not what you think. Many people think meditation requires you to sit crisscross applesauce and completely clear your mind. Those people tend to get frustrated quickly and quit altogether. Know why? Because it is impossible to actually clear your mind! The point of meditation is to slow down and be present with ourselves, which is precisely what many of us are afraid of. Anxiety occurs when you're worried about the future, and depression is often past-focused, so being more mindful and in the present moment can help improve our mental health.

The point of meditation is not to clear your mind, it's to notice your thoughts and see them as separate from yourself. If you're completely new to this, I know that may sound odd, but if you suffer from mental illness or engage in negative self-talk, learning that you are not your thoughts is very powerful. Headspace, an app dedicated to meditation training, helped me with this through a process called noting. During meditation, when you notice your mind has wandered off, simply note if the distraction is a thought or a feeling and then bring your mind gently back to your breath.

When I first started meditating, my thoughts went something like this: "I don't think I'm doing this right. Stop thinking. Ugh, now I'm thinking about thinking!" This is natural. We call meditation a practice for a reason. There is no such thing as a perfect meditation, but it will get easier with time. So, be gentle with yourself!

To begin meditation, sit down or lay somewhere comfortable and quiet, and set a timer for five minutes. Close your eyes and focus on your breath. If you notice a thought or an emotion, simply make note of it and return your focus to your breath.

There are tons of articles, books, apps and other resources to teach you how to meditate. If you're just starting out, Headspace and 10% Happier offer a free trial in their apps that walk you through the basics of meditation. You can also check out the Insight Timer app, which has tons of free meditations on a number of topics. I also love the Meditation Minis podcast with Chel Hamilton, which offers meditations for anxiety, sleep, confidence and overcoming negative thinking among other topics – and most are ten minutes or less. I personally enjoy picking out a meditation exercise that best fits my emotional needs based on the day.

There are tons of apps and types of meditation to explore, so try different variations until you find one that resonates. Be careful not to fall into the all-or-nothing trap of thinking you need to meditate for 30 minutes for the session to be effective. Even five minutes is better than nothing.

Silent Meditation

After doing guided meditation for several years, I discovered silent meditation, which is a powerful tool that allowed me to look even deeper within myself.

I first started silent meditation with a guided practice from the Tone It Up app. This particular meditation starts out with guidance. The instructor asks questions and guides you through breathing exercises in preparation for five minutes of silence. In silence, you drop deeper, past your thoughts, past your feelings and into the place where you feel completely at peace. Listen, I know this sounds woo-woo, but stay with me.

I know I've gotten to this place of stillness when outside sounds fade into the background and I feel calm and connected. Once there, I can ask for whatever I need, whether that be guidance, a question or a prayer I need answered.

Silent meditation helped me write the very book you're reading. Writing a book has been my dream since I was a little girl, but the topic and the subject matter has changed and morphed over time. When I started working with my coach and decided to dedicate my time to writing, I had no idea where to start or what to write about. I needed to find my story. I journaled and obsessed over it for several weeks. In silent meditation, I finally found the answer. I wanted to help other women to overcome their suffering from people-pleasing, perfectionism and anxiety. I awoke from that meditation so confident that this was the book I was supposed to write. I just knew.

If you're a spiritual person, you can think of silent meditation as a way to connect more deeply with God. If that's not your thing, think of it as your inner spiritual guide or your own intuition. You have all of the answers within you, you just have to be willing to dig deep enough to find them. Try it and see what happens. I double dog dare you.

To try silent meditation, sit in a quiet room. Use a pillow, a chair, or lay down on a yoga mat. Get comfortable and close your eyes. Focus on your breath, inhaling for a count of four, holding for a count of four and exhaling for another count of four. When you inhale, focus on spreading the breath throughout your lungs into your heart and stomach. Let it flow through to your arms and legs. When you exhale, picture any worries or concerns you have floating away like a helium balloon. If a distracting thought arises, notice it and release it on the exhale. To go deeper, you can picture a staircase and as you walk down each step, you sink deeper into your meditative state. Continue breathing until you feel a sense of peace. Once there, you can ask for guidance and listen to what comes through.

Try This: *Try both a guided and a silent meditation this week. Download different apps and test out different types of meditation practices to see what works best for you. Try meditation in the morning and before bed to see which time you prefer.*

Journaling

While meditation can help you separate yourself from your thoughts, journaling can help you examine thoughts and feelings on a deeper level. Writing things down, putting pen to paper, is powerful. Journaling uses both sides of the brain – the analytical left side and the creative right side – and can be extremely beneficial for your mental health.

If you're seeing a therapist, keeping a journal can help you relay any challenges you've faced since your last session. It can serve as a record of key milestones and can reveal how far you've come over time. Journaling can also bring you clarity, improve your mood and make you more aware of your thoughts and emotions and how they impact you. I often start a journal entry with a problem and find a solution by the time I finish writing.

As with any new habit, if you want to start a journaling practice, you need to create a routine and stick with it. I like to journal before bed as a way to reflect on my day, clear my mind and feel accomplished before going to sleep. I check in with myself, decompress and sort out my emotions from the day with my journal. It helps me to sleep better and start each day with a blank slate. Others prefer to start their day on a positive note with journaling. Try both and decide what works for you, then stick to it religiously.

When I started journaling, I committed to writing at least one page every night, even when I didn't feel like it. Now, I only journal a few nights a week, as needed, but consistency is key in the beginning in order to build the habit. After several months of daily journaling, I noticed significant improvements in my mood and mental health.

On days when I'm feeling less than inspired to start journaling, I use writing prompts to get the creative juices flowing!

- How are you feeling today? How do you want to feel? What is holding you back from feeling that way?
- List five things you are grateful for today and why. Try to incorporate at least one little thing that brightened your day and one big thing like a family member or your health.
- Why are you proud of yourself today?
- Who is someone you admire and why?
- Write a letter to your younger self.
- Review a book or movie.
- If you're struggling with negative thoughts, write them down, then examine them and reframe each one as a positive.
- Create three positive affirmations for yourself that you can use every day or when you are struggling
- How can you practice self-care tomorrow?
- What is one goal you can set for yourself for tomorrow? Make it specific, big enough to motivate you but also realistic and measurable. Include your "why" for setting this goal.

Try This: *Start a journaling practice this week using the above prompts. Try writing in both the morning and evening to find out which works best for you.*

The Brain Dump Method

When I have too many tasks, ideas and worries swirling around my head, I can't focus, let alone be productive. It feels like everything is a priority, yet nothing actually gets done.

Sound familiar? When I get overwhelmed like this, the brain dump is my go-to strategy to clear my head. By following these simple steps, you'll be able to clear your head and focus on what matters most. One day, one task at a time, sister!

1. Brain Dump

    First things first – get all of your thoughts out of your head and onto paper. Write down everything that's on your mind from critical tasks to ideas, thoughts, worries and everything in between. Don't worry about being organized, just let it all flow out in whatever order it comes to mind. Messy is good at this stage! You certainly can do this digitally, but I find actual paper helps me get organized and feel better.

2. Set Your Priorities

    Your priorities are personal. Only you know what's most important for you and what matters to your loved ones. Looking at your list, decide what your top three or four priorities or goals are for the week and write them down on a clean sheet of paper. We'll dig into priority and value setting in chapter eight, but for now, just focus on what your most immediate priorities are from this list.

3. Needs vs. Wants

    Take a look at your brain dump list. For the items that are tasks, choose two colors and categorize each item as "Need to Do" or "Want to Do" based on the priorities you've just outlined. For example:

    Need to Do:
    - Schedule doctor's appt
    - Make grocery list
    - Purchase birthday gift

Want to Do
- Call Mom to catch up
- Make nail appt
- Buy paint samples for kitchen

Be critical about what *needs* your attention and what is a *want*. I know I am guilty of putting pressure on myself for things that are not really necessary. Each need should have a deadline. You can also jot down how much time each task will take to help you prioritize.

Your "Want to Do" list, unlike your "Need to Do" list should be made up of things you truly desire to do. Visit your "want list" when you have free time or if you're feeling extra motivated or in need of some self-care. This is your "me time" list, and it could range from organizing your closet to learning how to knit or bingeing the latest Netflix series, whatever energizes you. Make sure you schedule some time for the things you want to do, not just the things you need to do. Time is a finite resource, so use it wisely!

4.   Process Thoughts and Worries

For the random thoughts you wrote down that are neither a need or a want, transfer them to another list or make a note to journal on them. I keep several lists in my iPhone Notes app for books I want to read, movies/shows to watch, things I want to research or purchase, writing ideas, and more. If you've written down any negative thoughts or worries, try a reframing exercise or journal to process them.

5.   Categorize

If you're feeling overwhelmed by the length of your "Need to Do" list, break down your tasks and categorize them to make it more manageable. Here are a few options:
- Highlight or star items that are urgent and which most closely align to your big picture goals and priorities and note items that can be deprioritized.
- Are there items on your list that you can get rid of by de-prioritizing or delegating to someone else? Remember, it's okay to ask for help!

- For larger tasks and goals like "get a new job," break them down into smaller steps, such as:
    o Update resume.
    o Reach out to three connections for referrals.
    o Apply to one job per week for four weeks.

After this step, your list likely looks like a hot mess. At this stage, I find it helpful to grab a blank piece of paper and copy the list in order of priority. I like to keep a weekly "Need to Do" list and move longer-term priorities to a separate "To-Do Later" list so they don't overwhelm me. This is a personal preference, but you may prefer to have everything in one list. Do what works for you.

Try This: Use the space in your workbook to try a brain dump.

Power Hour and Parking Lot

When I really need to focus at work or I want to bang out a bunch of "Need to Do" tasks, I use two methods to increase my productivity and efficiency: The Power Hour and The Parking Lot.

I first learned about the power hour from author and podcast host Gretchen Rubin. In her book, *Better Than Before*, Rubin introduces the "power hour" as a way to handle nagging tasks, by scheduling one hour to knock them all out at once. This can include answering emails, making phone calls and appointments, or cleaning the house. Set a timer for one hour and get moving! Do not allow yourself to be distracted from the tasks at hand until the timer goes off (Rubin, 2015).

You can also use a power hour to focus on one big task that needs your uninterrupted focus. I often use power hours to focus on my writing. Or, I'll put an hour on my work calendar to dedicate to a project I've been procrastinating.

It's important to limit distractions during the hour so you can be as productive as possible. Put your phone on "Do Not Disturb" or Airplane Mode and stay on task. I also like to set up a "parking lot."

You may have seen the parking lot used in meetings. If someone raises a good question or an idea that requires follow-up, but the idea doesn't fit within the current meeting focus, it gets added to the "parking lot" list. This list is used after the meeting for any follow-ups.

The idea here is the same. To stay focused on the task(s) at hand, place a blank sheet of paper and a pen to the side of your workspace. If another idea enters your mind, jot it down in the parking lot and re-focus on the task at hand. After your power hour, return to your parking lot list and decide if tasks are needs or wants.

My to-do list, like yours, is always a mile long and growing. We're constantly running around trying to do everything and be all things to all people, and our minds come up with tasks faster than we can tackle them.

I want to spend time with my friends and family, but when I do, I'm always thinking about the next task. Ironically, we're trying to please everyone by multi-tasking, but our relationships actually suffer from our lack of presence. By trying to make everyone happy, we often make no one happy, including ourselves. The strategies in this chapter can help you be more mindful and present in the moment.

Reflect: *How might you apply some of the strategies in this chapter to prioritize your mental health? How can you practice self-love for your mind?*

7. SELF-CARE FOR THE SOUL

With these new strategies in place to help you manage your physical and mental health, you can tackle the third piece of the self-love triangle: self-care.

Many brands are using the term "self-care" to market their products these days, but self-care is more than just face masks and bubble baths. Self-care is where physical and mental health intersect. It's preventative care for your body, mind and soul. Self-care is any activity that re-fuels your mental, physical and emotional energy. It fuels your tank and gives you the energy you need to face the mind monsters and daily stressors in your life. Self-care is about tuning into your emotional needs and nourishing your soul with things that make you feel good.

Did you know that when the gas tank on your car is below a quarter full, it takes more energy to run and is less efficient? The same goes for you, girl! If your energy tank is on E, running on the fumes of caffeine and sugar, it's time to fill up your tank with self-care. For those of you already telling yourself you don't have time – I'd like you to ask yourself if your car was on E, would you tell yourself you "don't have time" to stop for gas? Of course not! Your family, your boss and your friends do not want you to show up running on empty, they want your full presence, and that requires self-care.

While some say, "An apple a day keeps the doctor away," I like to say, "Self-care each day keeps burnout at bay." Just like we brush our teeth every day to prevent cavities, we need to practice self-care to prevent burnout – and this looks different for each of us.

Self-care is highly personal and can range from a workout to a nap, from painting to going out with your girlfriends. Introverts, like me, recharge with quiet time alone, while extroverts often need to connect with others to fuel up. Self-care can also depend on your likes and dislikes. As a creative person, any form of expression – writing, lettering, painting, etc. – helps me refuel. Chris on the other hand, de-stresses after a long day by playing video games.

But for those of you who fall into the Gen X category or later, you may not even know where to begin. Self-care is a fairly new concept. It was not something that my mom's generation or the ones before her talked about. If you have no idea what fills you up, I'd encourage you to use this chapter as a guide and run some experiments. Try out different self-care activities and see what makes you feel your best.

Foundational Self-Care: Sleep

Note: If you're a new mama, just go ahead and skip over this section and come back to it when that beautiful babe is sleeping through the night. Remember this is only a season and it will be over before you know it.

While self-care is highly personal, sleep applies to every single one of us. Sleep is the foundation of self-care. When you don't get enough sleep, you don't have the physical or mental energy to get through the day. For those of you that think you can run on 4 hours a night – you're wrong.

According to the Mayo Clinic, adults need a minimum of seven to nine hours of shut eye each night (Olson, 2019). You might already know this fact, but are you actually getting the recommended amount of sleep? Sleep is often the first thing we fall behind on when we're stressed, but it's the last thing you should skimp on.

According to Harvard Women's Health Watch (2006), there are several reasons why we should work on improving our sleep quality:

- Sleep helps you learn and remember new information through a process called memory consolidation.
- Sleep deprivation can cause weight gain by affecting the way our bodies process and store carbohydrates.
- Better sleep could improve your overall health, immune function and fight diseases like cancer.

- Sleep loss may result in irritability, impatience, inability to concentrate, and moodiness. We've all been there right? We are not our best selves when we are sleepy.

While many of us may try to compensate for poor sleep habits with a few extra hours on the weekend, research shows that you can't just "make up" for lost sleep (Depner et al, 2019). Research has suggested that a person would actually need four days of adequate rest to make up for even one hour of sleep debt (Kitamura et al., 2016). So, if you're not getting enough shut eye each during the week, it's nearly impossible to compensate for it on the weekend.

Create a Bedtime Routine

A bedtime routine can help signal to your brain that it's time to wind down. On weeknights, even if I'm working from home, Chris and I start getting ready for bed by 10:00 p.m. Setting a routine with your partner definitely makes things easier. Chris is often the one pulling me away from my laptop or phone at night, reminding me it's time for bed. At which point, I wash my face, brush my teeth and get into bed to do my nightly journaling.

Importantly, I have my phone set to go into "Do Not Disturb" mode after 10:00 p.m. to avoid distractions while I'm trying to sleep. I also charge my phone overnight on the other side of the room, which is one of the easiest but most impactful changes I've made to improve my sleep quality and help me wake up more easily.

If you have trouble sleeping, one of the worst things you can do is lie in bed scrolling on your phone. According to Harvard Health Publishing (2012), blue light, commonly found on electronic screens, suppresses melatonin, a hormone that influences your circadian rhythm, or internal body clock. Between the blue light, the stimulation and all the notifications, it's much better to grab a book than your phone when you're trying to fall asleep.

Try This: Create your own bedtime routine.

1. *Determine how much sleep you need to function optimally. For example, I find my body operates best on seven hours, but more than eight makes me feel groggy.*

2. *If you've been sleep deprived and aren't sure how much shut eye you need, experiment on the weekend. Note what time you go to bed and allow yourself to wake up naturally without an alarm clock. That's right, your homework is to sleep in! When you don't set an alarm, your body will automatically wake you up when it's well-rested at the completion of a REM cycle. Do this a few times and calculate your average hours of sleep.*

3. *Set your bedtime. What time would you need to go to bed to get the optimal amount of sleep for your current wake up time? Is this doable? Consider if you have room to wake up earlier than you already do to give yourself more time for you in the morning, whether it be to work out or to spend some quiet time alone before your family wakes up.*

4. *Write out your bedtime routine. What do you need to do before getting in bed and when do you need to start this routine in order to be ready for lights out? I also challenge you to add one new relaxing activity to your nightly routine. Could you journal for a few minutes? Try writing down what you're grateful for or reading a book. You could even try bedtime meditations. See what works best for you.*

Here's a quick snapshot of my own bedtime routine:

10:00 p.m. - start getting ready for bed.
- Phone automatically set to "Do Not Disturb" mode.
- Brush my teeth, wash my face, apply skincare.
- Lay out my clothes for the next day.
- Set my alarm and plug in my phone across the room
- Get in bed and journal.

10:30 p.m. - lights out, eyes closed

Falling Asleep

Now that you've established a bedtime routine to prepare your body for sleep, what about actually falling asleep? When you lay down and put your body to rest, does your mind kick into overdrive?

For me, insomnia began in my pre-teen years. I recall lying in bed, ruminating on all the things I had to do, scrutinizing things I'd said during the day (*did I upset my friend with the joke I made at lunch?*) or worrying about a test I had the next day (*did I study enough?*). Then I'd realize I wasn't asleep and calculate how many hours I could still get. I'd end up in tears over not being able to fall asleep, which of course made sleep even more elusive.

My first therapist taught me some breathing techniques that helped me to focus my mind into a relaxed state so I could fall asleep. Though I didn't realize it at the time, this was my first introduction into meditation and mindfulness (before it was trendy!) and these are strategies I still rely on today.

Ironically, the more you focus on trying to fall asleep, the more likely you'll stay awake. Instead, focus your brain on something specific, like breathing exercises, a story or something to memorize. This way, your brain relaxes, allowing you to drift off and catch some Zs. This strategy, developed by Luc Beaudoin, Ph. D., an adjunct professor at Simon Fraser University in British Columbia, is called cognitive shuffling (Burkeman, 2016). The idea is simple. Keep your mind busy by focusing on something else, rather than worrying about things you can't control at the moment. Here are a few of the strategies I use to fall asleep when my mind is wandering:

1. Breathe. It sounds simple, but if you just focus on your breath, sleep will come more easily. Practicing meditation during the day will help make this easier. Here are a few of my favorite breathing techniques to get you started:
    - Breathe in for four counts and out for four; repeat.
    - For a different technique, breathe at your normal pace and count your breaths. Inhale (1), Exhale (2), Inhale (3), Exhale (4) until you get to ten; repeat.
    - *Note: If a distracting thought comes up, simply draw your attention back to your breath. The point is not to "clear" your mind, just to focus it.*

2. Play Alphabet Soup. Choose a broad category like fruits and vegetables, animals or cities. Starting with the letter A, think of something in that category that starts with that letter, and continue through the alphabet. (i.e. Apple, Banana, Cauliflower, etc.). If you open your eyes, start over at A.

3. Test your memory. No joke, I learned the alphabet backwards while trying to fall asleep many years ago, and I can still recite it to this day. This one will only work until you complete the task, but it will likely take you several nights. You can do this with anything you are trying to memorize – as long as it doesn't make you get out of bed to check your notes!

4. Read a book. Try to avoid grabbing your phone or turning on the TV. Remember, anything with blue light can trick your mind into thinking it's daytime. Reach instead for a good book. Reading can transport you out of your own mind and into someone else's; it's like its own form of meditation.

5. Listen to music or a podcast. Pop in your air pods and listen to something you find relaxing. Since your phone can keep you awake, I recommend setting a sleep timer and leaving it across the room while you listen. Meditation apps like Insight Timer also offer sleep meditations, which can be great to play out loud for both you and your partner as you wind down at the end of the night. You could also try white noise or nature sounds if that's your thing!

6. Write it down. If you still have tasks or negative thoughts on your mind, write it down. Jot down a to-do list if you're worrying about all that needs to be done or journal for a few minutes if you're trying to work through an idea, thought or feeling. Since I started journaling, I've found sleep comes more naturally. Physically getting thoughts out of your mind and onto paper can help you put whatever it is to bed (literally!) for the night.

My husband can attest, I don't have trouble falling asleep anymore. He often jokes about how quickly I fall asleep at night. Once I kiss him goodnight, I'm snoring in no time. Because I learned these strategies early on in life, I know what to do when my mind races.
Getting enough sleep is the foundation of good self-care. If you aren't well-rested, you won't be at your best. While there will always be times when this isn't possible, you should prioritize proper shuteye whenever possible.

Self-Care Toolkit

With a solid foundation of a good night's sleep, you can start the day off right. If you're anything like me – and I think you are, if you've gotten this far – you go so fast checking off your to-do list, taking care of others and doing "all the things" that you rarely take a beat to think about what you need. When you don't pay attention to your own emotional needs, you can miss the signs that you need a break. When you miss these warning signs, you are on a one-way trip straight to burnout city.

When I started therapy again after college, I felt like I was stuck in a cycle of stress, denial and burnout. Every week looked the same. On Monday, I typically woke up feeling excited and motivated. I was busy at work, crushing my personal goals, working out, eating healthy and making time for friends and family. On Tuesday, I often needed an extra cup of coffee to start the morning, but I pushed through. It was a day full of meetings and trying to please others. On Wednesday, it became tough to get out of bed and by Thursday, I couldn't focus at work. I felt overwhelmed by the smallest tasks and by the end of the day, I was totally burnt out. I would skip my workout to lay on the couch, snap at my husband for something stupid, and drown my sorrows in sugar and two big glasses of wine. By Friday, I woke up feeling physically crappy from what I ate and drank the night before. I would mentally beat myself up for the tasks I didn't get done and feel ashamed for taking it out on Chris. Feeling depleted heading into the weekend, I had little energy to give to the people and things I loved. This cycle repeated nearly every week.

What's the point of working for the weekend when you're too exhausted to enjoy it? I thought I needed to learn how to manage my stress, but in reality, I just needed to make time for self-care. Stop waiting for Friday to do things that fill you up.

We move so fast during the work week trying to keep all of the balls in the air that we don't stop to take care of ourselves. We don't realize our own needs until they are screaming at us, which can damage our relationships and our health. But it doesn't have to be this way.

To help me prioritize my self-care, I created a daily self-care practice. I shared it on my blog and realized women everywhere needed this. So, I turned it into a more comprehensive self-care toolkit that you can customize and use every day to check in with yourself and better manage your emotions and stress. The full toolkit (included in your workbook) includes my three-step daily self-care practice, my six types of self-care menu and a customizable template for you to fill out.

3-Step Daily Self-Care Practice

It's important to check in with yourself daily to identify how you're feeling and what you need emotionally. I find this exercise most helpful after work, as that's the biggest stressor for me, and I want to bring my best energy into my personal time at home. You might need to check in every morning, on your lunch break or before bed. Try this three-step practice a few different times and see what works best for you.

1. Check in with yourself.

   Most conversations start with, "How are you?" But how often do we stop and ask ourselves that question and really listen to the answer? It's important to check in with yourself daily and ask yourself what you need. This concept is foreign to many of us.

   Ask yourself how you're feeling right now. You can use a list of feelings to help you find words for the emotions. My favorite is "The Feeling Wheel," developed by Dr. Gloria Wilcox (1982). The wheel breaks down our emotions into six main categories – mad, sad, powerful, peaceful, scared, and joyful – with more specific feelings under each category. For example, "scared" is broken down into feelings like "confused," "anxious," "helpless," "discouraged," and "embarrassed" among others. While you may feel a number of emotions, try to focus on the one that is most dominant.

2. Feel the Feels.

   Now, sit with your emotions for a few minutes. How does it feel? Where in your body do you experience the feeling? If helpful, you can journal on it. What is this emotion telling you to do right now? For example, if you're feeling sad, you might want to cry, lay down or eat a pint of ice cream.

Allow yourself to feel the emotion by giving in to one of these inclinations. Have a good cry if you need to, yell, scream or punch a pillow. Set a timer for 10-15 minutes and let it out. For the record, I don't recommend eating a whole pint of ice cream but giving in to the craving and eating a few scoops is more than okay! Remember: there are no bad foods, so give yourself some grace.

When talking to my Mimi about this topic, she echoed the importance of acknowledging difficult emotions and allowing ourselves to feel them. "You have to be sad sometimes or you won't know true happiness," she said. "You can't feel good all the time."

Pretending everything is fine won't make it true. If we push difficult emotions away or try to ignore them, it's only a matter of time before they bubble to the surface. It's part of the human experience to feel pain. We aren't supposed to be happy all the time. Allow yourself to experience negative emotions, but then move on.

"A good cry is the best thing ever," Mimi said, "but you can't wallow in it."

3.   Apply self-care.

Dry those tears and ask yourself, "How do I *want* to feel? What do I need to get there? How can I apply self-care to move forward with my day?" Take at least 10 minutes to take care of yourself.

Our emotions often push us to do the opposite of what we really need. When I'm anxious, I want to go, go, go. I keep myself busy, so I don't have to think about what's bothering me until I eventually crash. What I often need is to get away from the stressor and to take a quiet moment to walk or breathe. This idea is based on a DBT (dialectical behavioral therapy) technique called "opposite action" (Rollin, 2017). When I'm feeling down, I want to be alone, but what I really need is connection with friends and family.

To determine what type of self-care you need, I find it helpful to create a self-care menu. I like to divide self-care activities into six categories based on my emotional needs:

1. Comfort
2. Connection
3. Restoration
4. Distraction
5. Motivation
6. Release

In my own self-care menu, I've outlined activities that help satisfy each of these needs. You can find a printable version of my self-care menu and a customizable template in your workbook.

Try This: Make your own self-care menu by making a list of things that help you feel better in different situations. Reflect on the following prompts to guide you.

- *What comforts you when you are feeling anxious or down?*
- *Do you avoid connecting with others when you feel certain emotions? When do you most need connection?*
- *What restores your energy? If you're an extrovert this may overlap with connection as being around people fills your cup, while introverts need alone time to restore their energy.*
- *What are your favorite forms of distraction when you're worrying or sad about something? This may overlap with other categories like connection, or you might prefer a solo activity like watching Netflix or funny videos, reading a good book or cleaning the house.*
- *What motivates you? If your energy is low or you're overwhelmed, how do you get moving? It might be a walk, a brain dump, or setting a few small goals for the day.*
- *What helps you release negative energy? I find that working out is great for releasing anxiety and anger, but when I'm feeling sad or down, I like to journal to reframe my thoughts.*

Our needs are often the first to be compromised when our schedules get busy. What a lot of women don't realize is that when you neglect yourself, you aren't giving your best to those around you. We become resentful, depleted and anxious, and the people around us can feel it. You may keep giving, but your loved ones can feel when your heart isn't in it.

The key is to do this self-care practice intentionally every single day, until it becomes a habit. Eventually, you'll get better at noticing your emotions in real-time and being more mindful of your needs throughout the day.

Women have thousands of excuses for why we can't make time for ourselves. Whenever those thoughts creep in, remember why you started. When you take care of yourself, you have more energy for the people and goals you care about most.

Try This: *Stop what you're doing right now and set a daily alarm for a self-care check-in. Find the time that works best for you. I like to check in at 5 p.m., as a reminder to stop working and focus on myself before transitioning into my evening.*

Self-care keeps us mentally and physically strong so we can pursue our bigger goals and dreams. We need to make time for ourselves every single day if we want to show up as the best version of ourselves for our family, our friends and our future.

PART THREE: EMBRACE AUTHENTICITY

8. WHAT MATTERS MOST

We spent the last several chapters working on loving our body, mind and soul, because at the end of the day, we can't give our best to the people we love if we don't love ourselves first. When we don't love ourselves, we live for other people's approval and lose sight of our own values. We seek external validation, chasing goal after goal and reaching for gold stars of approval. But at the end of the day, we're left feeling empty.

Now that you understand how to prioritize yourself with health and fitness, mental well-being and self-care, you can evaluate and set priorities in other areas of your life. In this chapter, you'll outline your core values, and what and who matter most to you. In chapter nine, you'll create boundaries so you can protect the authentic life you've begun to build.

Values

Values are a set of principles or ideals that are unique to each of us (Tesic, 2017). They reflect who we are at our core. If you're a recovering people-pleaser, you may have lost sight of your personal values because you've been living by others' expectations for so long. But even if you're not aware of your values, you have likely felt the effects of misaligned values and actions.

When your actions don't match your values, internal conflict arises. You may feel unfulfilled in a job if it doesn't align with your values but stay in it because you think it's what you're supposed to be doing. You may not care for another person if her values are different from yours but seek her approval anyway because you want to be liked.

Your personal values are still within you, you may just have to dig a little deeper to find them. And that's exactly what this next exercise is designed to do.

Try This: To identify your core values, give yourself the time and space to dig deep.

1. Review the list of values in your workbook. Download it at workbook.strongcalmkelsey.com/download

2. Circle all the values that stand out to you as you go through the list. Don't overthink it. Just identify the words that feel important to you. This should be the easy part!

3. Next, narrow your list down by grouping the values together into categories that make sense to you. If you have three words that seem related put them together and choose one word that encompasses all three. It's easy to overthink this but remember it's more of an art than a science. There is no perfect answer, so tell that inner perfectionist to back off!

4. Combine and cross out values until you have it down to just two core values that are most important to you. If you have 10 values, you really have none, so try your best to whittle it down. What two things are most important to you to live a fulfilling life?

My two core values are "authenticity and "making a difference."

I value authenticity because I want to show up as my genuine self every single day. For me, that means being independent and creative, pursuing wellness and growth, while giving myself grace to just *be*.

My second core value is "making a difference." While authenticity is self-focused, making a difference is other-focused. I want to make a difference by showing love and compassion to my family, friends and the world around me. My greatest desire is to make an impact, to help others and to leave my mark on the world. But my value of authenticity ensures I stay grounded in who I am, rather than acting out of people-pleasing and perfectionism. For me, these values help me stay true to my heart.

Priorities

For the most part, our values don't change, but how we interpret and use these values may change over time because our priorities shift as we go through different seasons of life.

When I first graduated college, for example, I was working on my master's degree and working part-time with the goal of earning a full-time position at my company. During this time, I put more energy and time into work because it was a key priority for me.

However, after my company hired me full-time, I continued to work at the same pace, trying hard to prove my worth, when in reality I already had. My priorities needed to shift. I was newly married, and I was worried my stress was impacting my husband and our relationship. That's when I made the decision to prioritize my marriage, which required me to make my mental health a priority too, so I could show up as my best self for my husband.

When I decided to write this book, my priorities, again, had to change. I had to reorganize my day to give my best hours to writing, which for me is first thing in the morning. I decided to move my workouts to the evening, and I scaled back at work.

During this time, I was recommended for several job opportunities at my company, and I couldn't decide which one to pursue. As I detailed the different opportunities to my career coach, she said, "You just gave me a lot of reasons why none of these jobs are right for you, so what's the pull? Is it just flattery or is there something really exciting for you about one of these positions?"

This is why therapy and coaching are so valuable. Often others have the ability to see patterns you can't see alone. I was writing a book on people-pleasing and falling victim to it in the process. I realized I couldn't decide which job I wanted because I didn't want any of them. I was flattered that my boss and other colleagues would consider me for these roles, and I didn't want to let anyone down, but work wasn't a priority for me in this season. I had never not been career-focused, so it was strange for me to turn down what, on paper, were great opportunities. However, my dreams of writing a book took priority over work at that time, and I realized that was 100 percent okay.

Priorities change with the seasons of life and it's important for us to recognize these shifts and be intentional about how we spend our time.

Reflect: Now that you've identified your values, write down your biggest goals, dreams and desires – not what others want for you. What do you want? Dream big, nothing is off limits, so don't hold back. Close your eyes and think about what you want most in your life right now. What are you working towards? That is your priority in this season.

Look at the list below and add to it if necessary. Choose the top three that are a focus for you right now.

Career, Connection, Education, Family, Finances, Friendship, Growth, Health, Home, Love, Marriage, Parenthood, Relationships, Spirituality, Wellness, Other Personal Goals

---

When I first did this exercise, I had trouble prioritizing because at face value these are all really important things. But ask yourself, which area requires your main focus *right now*?

We cannot and should not prioritize all of these things at all times. Your top three should be for this season. It doesn't mean you don't care about the other things; it means that those areas may not receive as much attention right now.

I encourage you to return to your values regularly and evaluate your priorities against them as life's seasons come and go. If you are a new mom, parenthood is likely a high priority and your career may be lower on your list. But parenthood or family doesn't always need to be your number one. As your kids grow older, you may want to focus on other things. In a season where you need to focus on your career, you may need help in the parenthood department – from your partner, a family member or hired help. If you are looking for or starting a new job, your career may be a big focus for you right now. If you just got married or you're dating someone special, perhaps love is at the top of your list. Remember, you *can* have it all, but you can't do it all alone.

As recovering people-pleasers, it's also important to recognize the people who matter most and those who, well, frankly, don't matter. Motivational Speaker Jim Rohn said, "You are the average of the five people you spend the most time with," (Groth, 2012). Surround yourself with people you love and care about and ignore the haters. Prioritize the people who fill you up rather than those who drain your energy.

Try This: Make a list of all the people you love and care about most in your life. If you have a big family, don't worry about naming every third cousin, just list all the people you see and talk to regularly. Who is most important in your life?

Now, who are the five people whose opinions you value most? Who are the five people you can call on for advice, who are there for you and who in turn you want to be there for? If you were going to live on an island and could only take five people who would they be?

Number one on your list should always be yourself. As recovering people-pleasers, we need to proactively ask ourselves "What do I want? What do I need?" People-pleasing can cause us to lose ourselves, so it's important that we make a proactive effort to listen to ourselves.

This is a tough but really eye-opening exercise. It can feel a little harsh if you've been people-pleasing for a long time. For you 1990s babies, it's a lot like picking your "top eight" on Myspace – remember that drama? Except this list should be private. It's not meant to hurt anyone's feelings, but to help you prioritize the people in your life who you really value. Stop prioritizing people who don't do the same for you and whose opinions don't matter.

Reflect: Journal on how this exercise made you feel and what you discovered. Where are you putting in too much effort? It might be an overbearing relative, who you love dearly, but realize their opinion doesn't matter to you. Or maybe it's a friend who you jump through hoops for, but who doesn't do the same for you.

When I did this exercise, I struggled with how to include work. Should I include my boss on my people list? What about my business partners who contribute to my year-end review or my professional mentors? When I examined this further, I realized work doesn't belong on our people priority list. If you're new in your career, working towards a promotion or starting your own business, work may be a current priority for you. However, it's the job that is the priority, not the people.

Keep your list of values and priorities somewhere safe and return to it when you're feeling the people-pleaser come out. If you're trying to stretch and mold yourself to meet someone else's needs, ask yourself if it's aligned with your values and priorities. If someone needs a favor that is going to inconvenience you, are they someone who would do the same for you? It's not that all of your actions are to get something in return, but as people-pleasers we tend to overdo it. Recognizing who and what we value helps us prioritize what matters most in our lives.

9. PROTECTING YOUR NEW LIFE

Once you've done this tough work to outline your values, priorities and people, you can begin to build boundaries to protect your energy and time for the things that truly matter.

At its core, people-pleasing is a confusion of ownership and responsibility, a struggle to recognize where you end and someone else begins. If you're an empath like me this can be particularly difficult. Empaths are not only aware of other people's emotions, they absorb emotions. I feel deeply for other people. I cry regularly at movies because I can *feel* the characters' pain. When a loved one is struggling, I often struggle too, taking on their feelings and, by proxy, responsibility for them. As a recovering people-pleaser, I want to jump in and save everyone. I don't like to see anyone suffer, especially the people I love.

I love helping people and I'm sure you do too. It feels good to make other people feel good. However, when your happiness is reliant on other people's happiness and approval, it can become a problem. Other people's emotions are not your responsibility. We can do nice things and be a good person, but ultimately, we cannot control other people's reactions and feelings. You could give someone a million dollars and still not make them happy. Your happiness is *your* responsibility, and their happiness is *theirs*. Each of us has to do the inner work to be happy, the work you are doing right now. We can't do it for anyone else.

Boundaries can help us distinguish between what is our

responsibility and what is not. If you've been pleasing, perfecting and performing your whole life, the concept of boundaries is likely completely foreign – at least it was to me. In the book *Boundaries*, authors Dr. Henry Cloud and Dr. John Townsend finally explained it in a way that I could understand.

As human beings, we each have a daily load of responsibilities. Think of them as a pile of baseball-size stones you carry with you every day. These responsibilities may get heavy, but because each of us has our own load, we can't take on stones from other people. There are times, however, when we each are faced with boulders, big changes or difficulties in our lives, like the death of a loved one, the loss of a job, or illness. Boulders can't be carried alone. We need our support network to help us break them down. Help your people with their boulders, but don't take on their daily load (Cloud and Townsend, 2008).

"We have a responsibility to others but not for others," Cloud and Townsend say. In other words, we have a responsibility to help loved ones in need, but we are not responsible for other people's problems. That's why it's important to set boundaries for yourself on what you will and will not do for others (Cloud and Townsend, 2008).

Think of your boundaries as a fence around your house. Only your feelings, attitudes and beliefs exist within your property line, no one else's (Cloud and Townsend, 2008).

When we don't have clear boundaries, it is often because we're afraid of disappointing, angering or upsetting people. We take on responsibility for these emotions that doesn't actually belong to us, and as a result we leave our values and priorities unprotected. By setting boundaries we teach people how to treat us. You can build a gate in your fence, but *you* decide who goes in and out.

Let's take a look at boundaries in different types of relationships.

Boundaries in Families

Setting boundaries with your family can be particularly difficult. When we are children, our parents set boundaries for us in the form of rules in order to help us learn how to interact with the world. As we become adults and enter the world on our own, we have to start setting boundaries of our own (Cloud and Townsend, 2008). For example, your parents probably enforced a bedtime when you were young to ensure you got proper rest to grow and learn; but as you got older, they likely loosened these rules. As a teenager, you may have experienced the consequences of staying up too late before a big test at school, which taught you to set your own bedtime.

This example speaks to the importance of letting others (even family!) reap the consequences of their actions. As a teenager, my uncle got busted for underage drinking. His dad wanted to pay the fine and wipe his son's record, but my Mimi refused. She insisted that he pay for his mistake by completing community service – and he did! To this day, she holds that if they had simply paid the fine, he wouldn't have learned his lesson, and he might be on a very different path today. Mimi understands an important truth – that consequences, though they can hurt sometimes, ultimately help us make the changes we need to not repeat our mistakes.

When we see a family member struggling, we often want to rescue them. But if you don't let your loved one see the consequences of their mistakes; you are just slapping a band-aid on a bigger problem. If you continuously lend your brother money to get him out of debt, he will not feel the repercussions of his poor money management and he may take advantage of your lack of boundaries (Cloud and Townsend, 2008).

While parents need to set boundaries for their children, as we get older the opposite is true. A parent's job is to prepare you to enter the real world so you can build a life of your own. This can be a difficult transition for both the parents and the children because new boundaries have to be established and the traditional roles of the family need to change. As an adult child, with goals, needs and a family of your own, you need to set boundaries with your family of origin (Cloud and Townsend, 2008).

As an only child, I have always been very close to my parents. We have a great relationship that I cherish. However, as I moved out on my own and got married, I struggled with boundaries and guilt when I went home to visit. I tried to play the role of a kid living in their house again, while simultaneously trying to build my own life. The problem was that I was trying to keep things the way they used to be, while also building a new life with my husband. But you can't have both.

I learned to set boundaries by doing the things I wanted to do and saying no to the things I didn't want to do. Sometimes, that meant missing out on seeing a friend or missing a family event. I had to realize that I couldn't be all things to all people. You cannot be an independent, autonomous adult if we're still trying to be the baby of the family.

That also means holidays can no longer look the same. I have a husband and another family to visit and spend time with, and I often felt guilty for not being able to do everything and see everyone. This is a problem many adult children face as they build their own families. When I confided in my mom about my feelings of obligation and guilt, she told me that she too had struggled with this dilemma.

When I was a baby, my parents wanted to spend Christmas at home, just the three of us. My grandparents were disappointed at first, but if my mom had prioritized their feelings over our family's needs, she would have been the one to suffer. By explaining the reasoning behind her boundary and sticking to it, my grandparents adjusted, and my parents got their holidays at home. Those memories of me waking up at five a.m. with the wonder of Christmas and Santa Claus in our own home are ones I cherish. Those memories wouldn't have been possible without boundaries.

Boundaries at Work

Recently, one of my colleagues tragically and suddenly passed away. She was someone I had worked with at a surface level but whom I had never met. She was a fantastic partner, always willing to help. I was shaken up by the news, but I realized all I could say about her was that she was "nice." Something clicked for me in that moment that none of that mattered now. I hope she lived a full life. I hope she experienced love and joy. Most of all, I hope that she didn't neglect herself or the people she loved in order to be a good coworker to me or anyone else.

When I'm gone, I won't give a flying flip if my co-workers say how "nice" I was. At the end of the day, it's just a job. The sad truth is, if you leave your job tomorrow, you will be replaced and forgotten. I want people who truly know me and love me to feel like I was there for them, that I made their lives better just by being me.

I used to be a "yes woman," because I wanted everyone at work to like me. I wanted my co-workers to think I was good at my job and that I was a nice person that they enjoyed working with. But that is *not* your job. It's respect you should be seeking at work, not admiration. Energy spent worrying about what other people think is energy wasted.

There are undoubtedly some people you don't care for at work, but as a recovering people-pleaser, you probably still want them to like you. I've been there, but how ridiculous is that? We all have different personalities and it's human nature to disagree and have conflict. If you think your co-worker is a lazy SOB, then who gives a shit what he thinks of you? Not everyone will agree with you and not everyone will like you – and that's okay!

The first place to start with work boundaries is your job description. Filter incoming requests through your job duties, especially if they aren't from your boss. Here's a tip: if the email starts with "I need a favor," run! Learn to say "no" by offering an alternative solution, delegating to someone else on the team if it's relevant or by simply saying, "I don't have the time." Be firm when saying "no," rather than making excuses. An excuse gives the receiver the opportunity to respond, so if the answer is "no," be clear.

If you have a supportive boss, you can also lean on her for support in keeping you focused on the right tasks. If you need to, you can delay the requestor by saying you need to check with your manager and then let her step in. But, if you know the answer needs to be "no," don't put it off. You'll be surprised to see nothing bad happens and nothing falls apart when you set a boundary, making the next one even easier to implement.

Being busy and overwhelmed has come to be the marker of success in the corporate world. That's why it's important to set time boundaries. If you have clear working hours, stick to them. If you're salaried and have a bit more flexibility it can be easy to end up working non-stop, but remember you're not getting paid for those extra hours. Set working hours for yourself, just as if you were an hourly employee. Log off at night and try your best to stay off of email. This can vary depending on your line of work, but in my corporate office job, I know that if someone really needs me, they will call or text me. Most of the time, there is nothing truly urgent that justifies monitoring my email into the late evening.

By being open about your boundaries, you empower others to do the same, especially if you are a leader. Many parents with young kids at my company will leave a little early to get home and spend time with their kids. Do what works for you but be clear about your boundaries. Some of my coworkers are guilty of being on email late into the evening after their kids are asleep. *Guilty* is the keyword here! Though they take the initiative to leave work to be with their kids, they feel guilty and overcompensate by working all night to prove that they're doing their job. This can put pressure on other team members to be available in the evening too.

As someone without kids, I promise you I don't even bat an eyelash when parents leave work early. We get it, and when I have kids, I want to be able to do the same. If you need to log on at night, set a clear cut-off time (i.e. I put my laptop away at 8 p.m.) and discuss it with your team. The work will still be there tomorrow and there's likely nothing that needs your attention that urgently. If you're a leader, try not to send emails to your subordinates after work hours. You can schedule them to go out the next day or if you must send it, make it clear that a response can wait until the following day.

Whether you have kids or not, if you are working extra hours to get all of your work done, you are sending a signal that you *can* handle the amount of work you have, when in reality you cannot. If you find yourself burning the midnight oil regularly just to catch up, it may be time to examine your time management or talk to your supervisor about your workload.

If you work from home, boundaries can be even more challenging to set because work time flows into family and personal time. As I sit here typing, my company has been working from home for almost a year due to the COVID-19 pandemic. I am often on back-to-back Zoom meetings, with frequent interruptions from colleagues via text, IM, email and phone calls. Communication starts early in the morning and continues into the late evening with requests that often aren't urgent but feel critical to the sender. At first, I found all of this extra communication distracting and overwhelming. I couldn't get any work done because I was constantly being interrupted.

I started to practice boundary-setting by creating non-negotiables in my schedule. I wake up early to write before I log into email and start my workday. That is *my* time and it's not to be interrupted. I don't check email until 8:30 a.m.

Throughout the day, I block my calendar for important tasks that require focus and turn off email and phone notifications to limit distractions. If someone wants to meet with me, I share my availability, but I rarely make myself available immediately. I also schedule a break in my day to take a walk with my dog and clear my head. My lunch hour is sacred time, and I do what I can to protect it, rarely accepting a meeting invitation over the 12 o'clock hour. Lastly, I try my best to log off at 5:30 p.m. at the latest. One thing that helps me is to have something else I need or want to do. For example, I always work out from 5:00 to 6:00 p.m. and then start dinner. Knowing I need to get my workout in to be able to eat dinner motivates me to stop working.

It is not enough to set boundaries; you also need to communicate them.

One evening, I received a text from a co-worker at 10:00 p.m. asking me if I would present at a meeting four days later. I found both the method of communication and the time of this request to be highly invasive and unnecessary. I ignored the text and went to bed irritated. The next day, I pondered over how to respond. Should I text back or send an email? Should I ignore it all together? I knew I couldn't control this coworker's actions, but I could choose how to respond. Ultimately, I decided to send an email:

> *Hi Bob (name changed to protect the accused),*
>
> *I'm writing in response to your text message last night. I'm trying to set better work boundaries and not respond to messages after hours unless it's absolutely urgent. But that said, I'm happy to present at the meeting on Friday. Let me know the details.*
>
> *Thanks!*
> *Kelsey*

He replied almost immediately saying he was glad I didn't respond the night prior and that he needed to work on boundaries too. Mission accomplished. When I shared this example with my dad, he said he often sends messages like this after hours and doesn't think anything of it. I realized, for my generation, a call or a text message after hours feels invasive because we always have our phones on us. But for a Gen-Xer or older, a text message could be ignored just the same as an email could. My coworker didn't mean any harm, but setting my own boundaries helped him understand that it wasn't appropriate for me.

If you stick to a few cardinal rules at work, you will teach your co-workers how they can treat you and when they can expect a response from you.

Boundaries in Relationships

Early on in my marriage, I complained to my therapist about all of my responsibility. I was rushing home from work to make dinner, most nights feeling resentful and pissy the whole time. Though my husband would help with the cooking and cleaning, I had to ask him to do it and tell him exactly what to do. I felt like his mother instead of his wife.

My therapist helped me reframe this. A marriage is a partnership and we own the tasks 50/50. I was *choosing* to take responsibility for cooking and cleaning; no one was making me do those things. This was a big a-ha moment for me. My marriage did not have to look like my parents' or my friends' marriage. We had to build our own partnership, together.

I chose to take responsibility in my marriage for making dinner every night, because I realized that healthy eating and nutrition were more important to me than they were to my husband – and I made peace with that. This means I plan our meals, regardless of who cooks them. If he did the planning, we'd be eating hot dogs and grilled cheese sandwiches every night.

Through therapy and lots of practice, I learned to ask my husband for help at home. We often expect our partners to jump in and make dinner or clean the kitchen without being asked, and then we become resentful when they don't read our minds. Now, I embrace that cooking is one of my chosen responsibilities, but with one key shift. When I am running late from work or overwhelmed, I make a point to ask Chris to start dinner.

I also had to learn not to take responsibility for his reactions. Though he always agrees to help and is usually fine about it, sometimes he agrees with a heavy sigh or a sign of frustration. I had to learn not to overreact to that and not to snap, "Never mind, I'll just do it!" He is allowed to have bad days, or be moody about things, just as much I am. He doesn't have to be happy about helping me. The point is that he helps me because he loves me. We all have those days, but now you're just sharing the load.

You can also find ways to make these tasks easier to share. If you have all of the dinner recipes in your head, try writing them down and posting a menu on the fridge every week, so that anyone in your household can step in to help. One rule we've always stuck to is, if he cooks, I do the dishes and vice versa. Getting a grill was also a gamechanger because it made Chris excited to cook. Now, dinner is often a task we do together. He cooks the meat and mans the grill, while I prep the sides, and then we do the dishes and clean up together. Setting boundaries and learning how to ask for help has made our marriage so much stronger.

If you're feeling overwhelmed with household tasks, it may be helpful to sit down and have a conversation with your partner to divide them up evenly. You can start by writing household tasks and chores on post-it notes. Have a chore draft, taking turns selecting the tasks you will be responsible for. You can do this once a week, monthly or quarterly so you aren't stuck with one chore for the rest of your life!

This exercise will not only help you divide up the tasks more evenly, it will also open up a discussion about how your priorities and values may differ. You'll realize the things that matter to you, to your partner and the things that don't matter at all. If there are things that don't matter to either of you and truly don't need to be done, get rid of those post-it notes or reframe them. Perhaps you'll realize that having a fresh dinner on the table every night is something that stresses you out and that your partner doesn't really care about. Instead of forcing yourself to cook every night, can you make bigger dishes that can be split up over multiple meals? Could you meal prep on Sundays to lighten the load? Can you take turns cooking? As a recovering people-pleaser and perfectionist, this can be a helpful exercise in letting some things go. Once you have divided up the household tasks, you can focus on what's important and stop feeling resentful for what's not.

In my own marriage, I realized that many of the things I thought I was doing for both of us were really just for me. For example, I like to make the bed every morning. It helps me start the day right and makes going to bed at the end of the day more relaxing. Chris doesn't really care if the bed is made, and that's totally okay. It's *my* thing. When I realized this, I stopped huffing and puffing as I fluffed the pillows each day. Every once in a while, Chris does make the bed for me, and it makes me so happy because I know he's doing it just for me.

You don't have to be a 1950s sitcom housewife and a boss babe all at once. Marriage is a partnership, and you don't have to do it alone.

Boundaries in Friendship

Friendships can bring us great joy and fulfillment. However, without boundaries, friendships can feel draining, one-sided or dissatisfying. If you have a friendship like this, it's important to realize that *you're* the problem, not them.

Drs. Cloud and Townsend talk about two main ways boundaries can clash in friendships. The first is when both friends are people-pleasers (Cloud and Townsend, 2008).

On a trip to Disney World with my husband and my in-laws, we waited in line for three hours to ride the new Avatar ride at Animal Kingdom. About an hour into our wait, my husband, getting tired and hungry, announced something along the lines of, "This is ridiculous, I don't even want to ride this ride!" Soon we were all confessing that none of us actually cared enough to wait in the line, but we all thought we were doing it to please each other. *"I thought you wanted to ride it!" "No, I thought you did!"* In the end, we all shrugged and decided we had come too far to get out of line. This story makes me laugh because I realize now we all thought we were doing something for each other, when in reality we were all miserable. In the end, the ride was pretty cool, but the point is, don't assume you know what others want.

We each have to take responsibility for voicing our own opinions. You can only work on yourself. You can't change anyone else. Have you ever tried to plan a dinner with a friend and then gotten frustrated when they wouldn't voice a preference? In these types of relationships, both friends deny their own needs to keep the peace and please the other, but the result is often that neither of you are happy. You can voice your opinion without being overbearing. For example, when picking a restaurant, I often suggest a few options that sound good to me and ask my friend what suits her.

The second type of boundary issue in friendships is when a people-pleaser has a more aggressive, controlling friend. This is the friend who has no trouble voicing their needs and can often take advantage of a people-pleaser's time, belongings or kindness. Despite what you may think, the aggressive friend is not the problem, the people-pleaser is. By being compliant, you're enabling her to walk all over you. If any type of relationship is making you unhappy, you must take responsibility for those feelings and take action to fix the relationship or get out if it's not serving you. You need to learn to set clear limits and demand that they be respected (Cloud and Townsend, 2008).

In college, I had a roommate who was much more aggressive than me. Although we lived in a shared space, she seemed to only care about her own needs. She stayed up late with the light on when I was trying to sleep, she monopolized the refrigerator space and her boyfriend spent so much time at our place, he should've paid rent! These seem like such silly, normal college experiences now, but at the time I felt like my boundaries were being violated. I realize now the issue wasn't my roommate, it was that I hadn't set clear boundaries. Neither of us had lived with anyone other than family before, so it was up to me to communicate my needs. I never said a word about my concerns because I didn't want to upset her, even though I was suffering. Instead, I let these minor irritations fester until I eventually moved out and we ended our friendship. My friend likely didn't know how her actions affected me, and she may have benefitted from understanding how her behavior made me feel.

If you're in a friendship with an aggressive controller, it's important to set limits and communicate them clearly. These limits need to have consequences. For example, you could say, "If you don't respect my space, I'm going to have to move out." There are two possible outcomes to setting boundaries and clear consequences with your friends. Either the friend will realize how much they value the friendship and will take action to repair it, or you will both realize you're better off going your separate ways. While it can be sad to part ways with a friend, it is better than suffering in silence in a one-sided relationship (Cloud and Townsend, 2008).

It's still hard for me to set appropriate boundaries in my life, but I'm working on it every day. I was raised to be a "nice girl," and sometimes I'm afraid to set boundaries because I don't want to ruffle any feathers or hurt anyone's feelings. But the truth is, when you prioritize your own needs and start to set boundaries, you may hurt someone's feelings – and we need to learn to be okay with that. It is not your job to protect everyone's feelings – it's your job to protect your own. Read that again – I'll wait.

Reflect: Where do you need better boundaries in your life? In other words, in what areas of your life do you feel an imbalance? Are there specific people who consistently encroach on your boundaries? If so, what are some boundaries you can create and how can you communicate them to others?

10. WOMEN SUPPORTING WOMEN

Now that you have the tools to stop the endless cycle of pleasing, perfecting and performing in our own lives, we owe it to other women to share what we've learned. In this chapter, you'll learn how to recognize perfectionism and people-pleasing in others and how you can help support them.

How Are You Really?

During the 2020 coronavirus pandemic, I was struggling to keep up at work and I felt isolated while working from home. But I felt pressure to show up and be positive in every Zoom meeting. Nearly every call started with the question *"How are you?"* but I didn't think anyone really wanted to know. So, I gritted my teeth and said *"Good! How are you?"* Some days, saying "Good" was literally painful. Pretending to be fine zapped all of my energy.

However, when someone took the time to ask authentically, *"How are you doing with everything? How's your workload?"* I felt safe enough to open up. That permission led to some really helpful conversations with coworkers. The coworker on the other end would often open up about their similar struggles, and we'd swap stories and strategies. These conversations made me feel less alone and helped me be more optimistic as a result.

As women, we owe it to each other to keep an eye out for fellow perfectionists and call out their bullshit. If a friend says she is "fine" and changes the subject, ask her, *"How are you really?"* or open up to her first. Remind your girlfriends that you are here for them. Acknowledge them, show compassion and be empathetic.

In order to lead the way for other women, we need to start by being open and real. When one woman is brave enough to say, "I'm struggling," it gives others the permission to do the same. It's freeing not to have to pretend. Find at least one woman in your life that you can open up to – your mom, your best friend, a co-worker, or your favorite aunt.

Toxic Positivity

Naysayers will argue that complaining doesn't do any good, and that a positive mindset is the key to a happy life. While I agree that complaining alone won't solve your problems, there is a difference between being negative and being real. Negativity is complaining for the sake of complaining without any hope that things can change. A realistic optimist on the other hand, recognizes that a situation is difficult but has hope and motivation to change. Hiding behind a positive mindset philosophy only perpetuates the problem. Insisting that things are "fine," closes you off from changing and improving the situation and your life.

This toxic positivity is everywhere we look from self-help books to our friends and family (Scully, 2020). Have you ever opened up to someone only to hear "Just be positive!" in return? This is not only unhelpful, it's completely invalidating. Hearing this makes us reluctant to share again, so don't be that person. You don't always have to try to "fix" things for other people. Don't assume the person wants your advice unless they ask for it. Sometimes all you need is validation to feel better. Simply acknowledging the other person is a great start. *"I hear you," "That sounds really hard"* or *"I'm here for you"* are a great start. Part of being human is suffering, and we need support to get through challenging times in our lives. We need to know we aren't alone in the challenges we face.

Stop Judging, Start Supporting

Being authentic and giving other women the opportunity to do the same also means we have to stop judging each other. As recovering people-pleasers, we most often judge women that have learned to set clear boundaries in their lives, because we are envious. Judging others is often a reflection of what's going on in our own world. We criticize the woman who makes going to the gym a priority because we tell ourselves we don't have time. We judge the woman who gets a promotion or who is pursuing a personal goal because we don't prioritize our own goals. We say things like, *"Must be nice to have so much free time,"* or we call her selfish behind her back. For many of us, our biggest fear is that if we focus on ourselves even for an hour a day people will think we are selfish.

Ladies, this is important, so listen up. It is not selfish to take care of yourself. Judging women for their self-care perpetuates the "perfect" standard that we must be completely selfless to be a good wife, mom, etc. Let's start building each other up instead of tearing each other down, okay?

Try This: *Ways to support other women:*

- Ask, *"How are you doing?"* and mean it.
- Don't take "fine" for an answer if you suspect she's not. Asking *"How are you really?"* or *"Are you sure?"* can help.
- Open up first if necessary, tell her about a challenge you're facing.
- If a woman opens up to you, don't immediately jump to your own experience. This can feel like "one-upping." Listen first, ask questions and respond with empathy.
- Offer empathetic statements like, *"I'm sorry you're dealing with this." "That sucks." "That's really hard." "I hear you." "I understand." "I'm here for you." "How can I help?"*
- Don't invalidate her by saying someone else has it worse. Someone else's struggle does not minimize hers.
- Don't offer advice unless asked. Try *"Can I make a suggestion?"* or *"Do you want my advice?"*
- Don't tell her to *"Just be positive!"*
- If you catch yourself judging a woman, ask yourself why.
- Invite another woman you admire (or judge!) to coffee and find out her secrets to success.
- Compliment another woman and ask her for advice. *"I noticed you've been working out and I've been trying to make exercise a priority. Do you have any advice?"*

Notice how often you and other women gossip about others and make a conscious effort to stop. If someone is passing judgment on another woman, try to reframe it with compassion or an alternate viewpoint and change the subject. For example, if a friend says, "I can't believe Susan didn't volunteer for the bake sale!" You could say something like, "I'm sure she had a good reason. Honestly, I wish I hadn't volunteered this time, I took on too much this week." Let's normalize saying no, setting priorities and enforcing boundaries. Let's applaud other women for paving a path for us rather than tearing them down.

Instead of talking shit about the woman who seems to have it all together, ask her out for coffee and chat her up. You may learn something from her, or you may realize she needs support, too and you can support each other. It's okay to be vulnerable and open up to people about your struggles. I'm willing to bet she hasn't always been this way and she has her own story to tell, or maybe you'll find she's been pretending this whole time. Opening up to her may give her permission to be vulnerable and real. Who knows? She could become your new accountability partner or the friend you didn't know you needed.

We need to support each other in order to change the standard for the next generation of women. The more we open up to each other, the easier we can overcome perfectionism together. We have to stop pretending to have it all together and acknowledge that the current perfect standard we've been chasing isn't realistic.

Reflect: Who in your life could use your support? How can you open up to them and give them space to be authentic? Who do you judge most often and why do you think that is? Is she doing something you wish you could? How can you reframe your judgments as positives? Could you reach out to her for advice?

CONCLUSION: PASS IT ON, SISTER

Today, I'm strong, calm and more confident than I've ever been, but I'm not perfect.

It's important to acknowledge that while I'm the happiest I've ever been, I don't have it all figured out. I'm still a work in progress. I am a recovering people-pleaser and perfectionist, and much like an addict, it is something I will fight my whole life. But I finally realized – and I hope you do too – that my authentic life is *worth* fighting for.

Today, when the mind monsters say, *"Who do you think you are?"* I respond confidently, *"I'm a bad ass bitch who can do anything I put my mind to"* – and so are you.

My hope is that my stories and the strategies I've learned along my journey have opened your eyes to how people-pleasing and perfectionism are impacting you and how you can take action to change your life for the better.

The only way we can stop this endless cycle of pleasing, perfecting, performing and chronic burnout – is to change the narrative. This requires us to recognize that the current standard – the perfect, selfless woman that we've created in our minds – isn't realistic. We have to band together to denounce this ideal and build a new one for us, for our daughters and for the next generation of women.

The first step to changing any problem is to understand the root cause. In part one, we learned why women are more prone to people-pleasing and perfectionist behavior. Women are raised to be kind, generous "nice girls." We care too much about what other people think, we hold ourselves to impossible standards, and we put everyone else's needs before our own. The problem is that by pursuing selflessness as the gold standard we actually start to lose sight of ourselves. Neglecting our own needs over time can ultimately lead to anxiety, depression and burnout. While we can blame societal standards for making us this way, we have to take responsibility for fixing this problem ourselves.

When you realize that the real problem isn't "them" it's you, you can start to take back control of your life. We learned about the various mind monsters in our heads – impostor syndrome, guilt and shame, and sensitivity – and how to fight back with vulnerability and self-love.

In part two, we explored how to love ourselves from the inside out. Respecting our bodies with nutrition and exercise gives us the energy and health to do all the things we want to do for ourselves and for others. Prioritizing our mental health gives us the strength we need to keep going in times of adversity; and being open with others about our mental health gives them permission to do the same. Self-care is the final piece of the self-love triangle. It's preventative care for your mental and physical health, and it is absolutely essential to maintaining your wellbeing.

With these new self-love practices in place, in part three we examined our personal values and set new priorities and boundaries, which you may have lost sight of in your efforts to please others. Values are ideals that make up who we are; they are highly personal and individual. Priorities are the things we care about most in a particular season of life. Boundaries are the rules and guidelines we put in place in order to protect these values and priorities. Boundaries allow us to distinguish between what is our responsibility and what is not. We must set boundaries with our family, our loved ones, our coworkers and our friends if we want to change our lives.

Finally, we talked about how to support other women who are struggling. As you start to rebuild an authentic life for yourself, you will start to notice the patterns of pleasing, perfecting and performing in other women. When you spot another recovering perfectionist, ask her how she's doing, invite her to coffee, and support her through the journey. Vulnerability is the antidote to the impossible "perfect" standard we've been holding ourselves prisoner to. We have to be real with each other and we have to stick together.

I said from the beginning that this was not a quick fix or a "five easy steps to happiness" kind of book. Self-love is a lifelong journey, and it takes consistent practice. These strategies are ones that you can come back to over time when you need them. I wrote this book because I was sick of struggling and seeing the women around me struggle, too. If you've taken one thing from these pages, I hope it's this: being your authentic self is more than enough.

I hope as you turn this last page, you'll be inspired to pass this book on to other women in your life. Gift it to a new graduate or a friend on her birthday. Share it with your mom, your sister, your niece and when the time comes, share these concepts with your daughter. I want this book to be one that's passed on from woman to woman. The only way we can change the standard for future generations is by changing our own lives and passing it on. Every woman deserves to love herself fully – and it starts with you.

WHERE DO WE GO FROM HERE?

I hope this book has given you the resources, tools and the kick in the ass you need to start living life on your own terms. I hope it gives you the confidence that it *is* possible to break free from the endless cycle of pleasing, perfecting and performing.

If you haven't yet, now is a great time to download the free workbook, which will take you through the key points, exercises and journal prompts from each chapter. If you are serious about changing your life, this step is critical. Get your copy at workbook.strongcalmkelsey.com/download.

If you want to take things a step further, visit StrongCalmKelsey.com and subscribe for updates. I'd also love to connect with you on Instagram @StrongCalmKelsey or Facebook.com/strongcalmkelsey, where I share more content on mental health and my journey as a recovering perfectionist and people-pleaser. You can also contact me via email at strongcalmkelsey@gmail.com.

If this book helped you in some way, I'd love to hear about it. Honest reviews help readers find the right book. I also encourage you to share the book with the women in your life who might benefit from it. Let's change the perfect standard together.

xoxo,
Kelsey

ABOUT THE AUTHOR

Kelsey Buckholtz is the founder of StrongCalmKelsey.com, a blog dedicated to helping women be stronger, calmer and authentically themselves. Kelsey has a master's degree in communication from Rutgers University and a bachelor's degree in public relations from Penn State University. She works in corporate communications and resides in Lawrenceville, NJ with her husband, Chris, and their beagle chihuahua Zoe. *Strong, Calm, Confident You* is Kelsey's first book. Sign up for her email list at strongcalmkelsey.com.

NOTES

Chapter One

- Mark, D. (2017, March 2). *12 Stats About Working Women | U.S. Department of Labor Blog*. U.S. Department of Labor Blog. https://blog.dol.gov/2017/03/01/12-stats-about-working-women

- Frost, R. O., Marten, P., Lahart, C., & Rosenblate, R. (1990). The dimensions of perfectionism. *Cognitive Therapy and Research, 14*, 449–468.

- Flett, G. L., Hewitt, P. L., Blankstein, K., & O'Brien, S. (1991). Perfectionism and learned resourcefulness in depression and self-esteem. Personality and individual differences, 12, 61-68.

- Nealis, L. J., Sherry, S. B., Sherry, D. L., Stewart, S. H., & Macneil, M. A. (2015). 19 Toward a better understanding of narcissistic perfectionism: Evidence of factorial validity, 20 incremental validity, and mediating mechanisms. Journal of Research in Personality, 57, 11-25.

- Yiu, M. (2019, January 3). *People-Pleasing Versus Generosity*. Women's Therapy Institute. https://womenstherapyinstitute.com/people-pleasing-versus-generosity/

- Cedars Sinai Staff. (2019, February 13). *The Science Behind Random Acts of Kindness*. Cedars-Sinai. https://www.cedars-sinai.org/blog/science-of-kindness.html

Chapter Two

- *Guilt vs. Shame [Infographic] - NICABM*. (2017, June 15). NICABM; National Institute for the Clinical Application of Behavioral Medicine (NICABM). https://www.nicabm.com/guilt-vs-shame/

- Aron, E., & Aron, A. (1997). Sensory-Processing Sensitivity and Its Relation to Introversion and Emotionality. *Journal of Personality and Social Psychology*. http://www.hsperson.com/pdf/JPSP_Aron_and_Aron_97_Sensitivity_vs_I_and_N.pdf

Chapter Three

- InformedHealth.org. (2006). *Depression: What is burnout?* National Center for Biotechnology Information. https://www.ncbi.nlm.nih.gov/books/NBK279286/

- Mayo Clinic Staff. (2020, November 20). *Job burnout: How to spot it and take action*. Mayo Clinic. https://www.mayoclinic.org/healthy-lifestyle/adult-health/in-depth/burnout/art-20046642

- Are You at Risk of Burnout? Quiz: strongcalmkelsey.com/burnout-quiz/

Chapter Four

- Body for Life: transformation.com

- Workouts to try: Toneitup.com, thefitnessmarshall.org, LaurenGleisberg.com, Beachbody.com

- Nunez, K. (2019, July 10). *Working Out in the Morning: 13 Benefits, Research, Tips, and More*. Healthline; Healthline Media. https://www.healthline.com/health/exercise-fitness/working-out-in-the-morning#should-you-eat

- Weightwatchers: ww.com

- My Fitness Pal App: myfitnesspal.com

- Lauren Gleisberg Macro Book: laurengleisberg.com/product/macro-book/

- Kadey, Matthew. "Sugar Smarts: Added Sugars Are Everywhere-threatening Our Health in Countless Ways.

Use These Tips to Limit Your Sugar Intake." *American Fitness*, Vol. 36, No. 2, Spring 2018, Pp. 63–65. *Ebscohost*.

- Grace, Anthony A. "Dysregulation of the dopamine system in the pathophysiology of schizophrenia and depression." *Nature reviews. Neuroscience* vol. 17,8 (2016): 524-32. doi:10.1038/nrn.2016.57

- Fitlicity: fitlicity.com

Chapter Five

- Mayo Clinic Staff. (2018, May 4). *Anxiety disorders - Symptoms and causes*. Mayo Clinic. https://www.mayoclinic.org/diseases-conditions/anxiety/symptoms-causes/syc-20350961

- Nunez, K. (2020, February 21). *Fight, Flight, or Freeze: How We Respond to Threats*. Healthline; Healthline Media. https://www.healthline.com/health/mental-health/fight-flight-freeze#examples

- Penn State Dance Marathon: thon.org

- Online and Virtual Therapy Resources: betterhelp.com, talkspace.com

Chapter Six

- Katie, B. (2002). *Loving What Is*. Harmony. thework.com/books/

- Byron Katie's "The Work": thework.com

- NCCIH. (2016). *Meditation: In Depth*. NIH.Gov. https://www.nccih.nih.gov/health/meditation-in-depth

- Meditation Apps: headspace.com, tenpercent.com, insighttimer.com, meditationminis.com

- Rubin, G. (2015). *Better Than Before*. Broadway Books. Gretchenrubin.com

Chapter Seven

- Olson, E. (2019, June 6). *How many hours of sleep are enough?* Mayo Clinic. https://www.mayoclinic.org/healthy-lifestyle/adult-health/expert-answers/how-many-hours-of-sleep-are-enough/faq-20057898

- Harvard Women's Health Watch (2006). Importance of Sleep: Six Reasons not to Scrimp on Sleep. 2006. https://www.health.harvard.edu/press_releases/importance_of_sleep_and_health.htm

- Depner, C., Melanson, E., Eckel, R., Stothard, E., Morton, S., Wright Jr., K., Snell-Bergeon, J., Perrault, L., Bergman, B., Higgins, J., & Guerin, M. (2019). Ad libitum Weekend Recovery Sleep Fails to Prevent Metabolic Dysregulation during a Repeating Pattern of Insufficient Sleep and Weekend Recovery Sleep. *Current Biology*. https://www.cell.com/current-biology/fulltext/S0960-9822(19)30098-3

- Kitamura, S., Katayose, Y., Nakazaki, K., Motomura, Y., Oba, K., Katsunuma, R., Terasawa, Y., Enomoto, M., Moriguchi, Y., Hida, A., & Mishima, K. (2016). Estimating individual optimal sleep duration and potential sleep debt | Scientific Reports. *Scientific Reports*. https://www.nature.com/articles/srep35812

- Harvard Health Publishing. *Blue Light Has a Dark Side*. May 2012, www.health.harvard.edu/staying-healthy/blue-light-has-a-dark-side.

- Burkeman, O. (2016, July 15). Shuffle your thoughts and sleep | Health & wellbeing | The Guardian. *The Guardian*. https://www.theguardian.com/lifeandstyle/2016/jul/15/shuffle-thoughts-sleep-oliver-burkeman

- StrongCalmKelsey Self-Care Toolkit: strongcalmkelsey.com/self-care-toolkit

- Wilcox, G. (1982). The Feeling Wheel: A Tool for Expanding Awareness of Emotions and Increasing Spontaneity and Intimacy. *SAGE Journals.* https://journals.sagepub.com/doi/abs/10.1177/036215378201200411

- Rollin, J. (2017, March 9). *Feeling an Urge and Then Doing an "Opposite Action" | Psychology Today.* Psychology Today. http://psychologytoday.com/us/blog/mindful-musings/201703/feeling-urge-and-then-doing-opposite-action

Chapter Eight

- Tesic, S. (2017, August 18). *The Power of Personal Values.* Thrive Global; Thrive Global. https://thriveglobal.com/stories/the-power-of-personal-values/

- Groth, A. (2012, July 24). Jim Rohn: You're the Average of The Five People You Spend the Most Time With. *Business Insider.*

Chapter Nine

- Cloud, H., & Townsend, J. (2008). *Boundaries.* Zondervan. boundariesbooks.com

Chapter Ten

- Scully, S. M. (2020, July 22). *"Toxic Positivity" Is Real - and It's a Problem During the Pandemic.* Healthline; Healthline Media. https://www.healthline.com/health/mental-health/toxic-positivity-during-the-pandemic

Made in the USA
Middletown, DE
26 May 2021